T0373619

Heritage, Memory and Identity in Postcolonial Board Games

Heritage, Memory and Identity in Postcolonial Board Games is a unique edited collection that explores the interplay of heritage, memory, identity and history within postcolonial board games and their surrounding paratexts. It also examines critiques of these games within the gamer communities and beyond.

Drawing on a range of international contributions, examples and case studies, this book shows how colonialism-themed games work as representations of the past that are influenced by existing heritage narratives and discourses. It also considers the implications of using colonial histories in games and its impact on its audience, the games' players.

Heritage, Memory and Identity in Postcolonial Board Games will be relevant to scholars and postgraduate students in the fields of game studies, game design or development, heritage studies, postcolonial criticism, media studies, and history. It will also be beneficial to practicing game developers.

Michal Mochocki, Ph.D. in Literature and Dr. habil. in Culture and Religion Studies, explores storyworlds, narratives and role-plays in games, reenactment, and fiction from the angles of transmedia narratology and heritage studies. His recent book is *Role-play as a Heritage Practice* (Routledge, 2021). With grant funding from the National Science Center in Poland, he currently runs a research project on historical settings as transmedia storyworlds across literature and games. Outside the Academia, he was a writer and designer of historical larps and tabletop RPG, and a board game design educator with Rebel.pl. Now he works in video games with the False Prophet studio as a game writer, historical consultant, and R&D project manager.

Heritage, Memory and Identity in Postcolonial Board Games

Edited by Michal Mochocki

Routledge
Taylor & Francis Group

LONDON AND NEW YORK

First published 2024
by Routledge
4 Park Square, Milton Park, Abingdon, Oxon OX14 4RN

and by Routledge
605 Third Avenue, New York, NY 10158

Routledge is an imprint of the Taylor & Francis Group, an informa business

© 2024 selection and editorial matter, Michal Mochocki; individual chapters, the
contributors

British Library Cataloguing-in-Publication Data
A catalogue record for this book is available from the British Library

Library of Congress Cataloging-in-Publication Data
Names: Mochocki, Michal, editor.
Title: Heritage, memory and identity in postcolonial board games / Edited
by Michał Mochocki.
Description: Abingdon, Oxon ; New York, NY : Routledge, 2023. | Includes
bibliographical references and index. | Summary: "Heritage, Memory and Identity
in Postcolonial Board Games is a unique edited collection that explores the interplay
of heritage, memory, identity and history within postcolonial board games and their
surrounding paratexts. It also examines critiques of these games within the gamer
communities and beyond. Drawing on a range of international contributions, examples
and case studies, this book shows how colonialism-themed games work as representations
of the past than are influenced by existing heritage narratives and discourses. It also
considers the implications of using colonial histories in games and its impact on its
audience, the games' players. Heritage, Memory and Identity in Postcolonial Board
Games will be relevant to scholars and postgraduate students in the fields of game studies,
game design or development, heritage studies, postcolonial criticism, media studies, and
history. It will also be beneficial to practicing game developers"-- Provided by publisher.
Identifiers: LCCN 2023006771 (print) | LCCN 2023006772 (ebook) | ISBN 9781032411118
(hardback) | ISBN 9781032411125 (paperback) | ISBN 9781003356318 (ebook)
Subjects: LCSH: Board games--History. | Board games--History--Case studies.
| Board games--Design and construction. | Postcolonialism. | Collective
memory. | Group identity.
Classification: LCC GV1312 .H52 2023 (print) | LCC GV1312 (ebook) | DDC
794--dc23/eng/20230516
LC record available at https://lccn.loc.gov/2023006771
LC ebook record available at https://lccn.loc.gov/2023006772

ISBN: 978-1-032-41111-8 (hbk)
ISBN: 978-1-032-41112-5 (pbk)
ISBN: 978-1-003-35631-8 (ebk)

DOI: 10.4324/9781003356318

Typeset in Times New Roman
by KnowledgeWorks Global Ltd.

Contents

Contributors

Giaime Alonge is a Professor of Film Studies at the University of Turin, Italy. He has been Fulbright visiting professor at the University of Chicago. His main research areas are Hollywood cinema, Italian cinema, screenwriting, film and history, game studies.

Núria Araüna-Baró is an Associate Professor and researcher at Universitat Rovira i Vigili (Spain). She holds a Ph.D. in Communication and is a member of the ASTERISC Communication Research Group. She has a BA in Media Studies, a BA in Anthropology, and an MA in Creative Documentary. Her current research focuses on the representation of recent memory and activisms (mainly social movements and feminist strategies) in non-fiction genres and new audiovisual formats.

Miguel A. Bastarrachea Magnani holds a Ph.D. in Physics and a Ph.D. in Philosophy from the National Autonomous University of Mexico (UNAM). His interests lie in several fields, such as Quantum Physics, German Idealism, Philosophy of Symbol and Myth, and RPG studies.

Alexander Carneiro is a game designer and a Professor of Game Design and Media Production at Universidade Federal do Cariri, in Juazeiro do Norte, Brazil. He has a Master's degree in Communication from Universidade Federal da Paraíba.

Thiago Falcão is a Professor of Communication and Digital Media at Universidade Federal da Paraíba, in João Pessoa, Brazil. He holds a Ph.D. in Contemporary Culture and Communication from Universidade Federal da Bahia. His research interests are related to how politics interlace with gaming culture and its political economy.

Riccardo Fassone is an Associate Professor of Digital Media and Video Game History at the University of Torino, Italy. His areas of interest are Italian popular culture, with a focus on games and playful practices, and the history and theory of video games. As a game designer he has worked on several digital and analog games.

Juan Luis Gonzalo-Iglesia is an Associate Professor of the Department of Communication Studies at Universitat Rovira i Virgili and a member of the ASTERISC Communication Research Group. He holds a Ph.D. in Communication, a BA in Geography and History, and a BA in Journalism. His latest works focus on the representation of historical processes and conflicts through board games and the application of game experiences in education.

Andrew Kemp-Wilcox is an Assistant Professor of Practice specializing in Game Studies at The University of Arizona School of Information. He holds a Ph.D. in Communication from Georgia State University, and is a former narrative designer, game designer, and producer in the videogame industry. His research focuses on narrative games and the physical and embodied ways in which players perceive and co-constitute story and meaning.

Natàlia Lozano-Monterrubio is a Serra Húnter fellow at Universitat Rovira i Vigili (Spain). She holds a Ph.D. in Communication and is a member of the ASTERISC Communication Research Group. She has a BA in Advertising and Public Relations, an MA in International Public Relations, and an MA in Training for Teachers of Secondary Education. She is interested in analyzing the application of game experiences in education to foster motivation and creativity.

Michal Mochocki is an Associate Professor in Department of Anglophone Literatures at Kazimierz Wielki University in Bydgoszcz, Poland. He holds a Ph.D. in Literature and Dr. Habil. in Culture and Religion Studies. He explores storyworlds, narratives and role-plays in games, reenactment, and fiction from the angles of transmedia narratology and heritage studies. His recent book is *Role-play as a Heritage Practice* (Routledge, 2021).

Anna Sivula (Ph.D.) is a Professor of Cultural Heritage Studies and the Head of the School of History, Culture and Arts Studies at the University of Turku, Finland. She is a historian and historiographer, and she has researched the historical identity work in cultural heritage communities. Her research interests are industrial heritage, urban heritage, and game cultural heritagization.

Maurice W. Suckling holds a Ph.D. in Creative Writing from Newcastle University, and an MA in Global History from the University of Birmingham. He is an Assistant Professor in the Games and Simulation Arts and Science program, at RPI. He has written for over 50 published video games, including *Borderlands: The Presequel*, and designs board games.

Jaakko Suominen (Ph.D.) is a Professor of Digital Culture and Dean of the Faculty of Humanities at the University of Turku, Finland. In his studies, he has focused on the cultural history of information technology and the history of media and technology. He has also studied the history of board gaming as well as various forms of uses of history within game cultures.

1 An Introduction to Board Games in Postcolonial Game Studies

Michal Mochocki

Introduction

This collection is a new contribution to postcolonial game studies, extending the debate to nondigital board games. The postcolonial approach is relatively new in game studies: its first book-length publications came out in the late 2010s. So far, this field has been dominated by digital games. Board games are studied in a few chapters in *Postcolonial Perspectives in Game Studies* (edited by Mukherjee & Hammar, 2018), and occasionally mentioned in Mukherjee (2017). They are repeatedly featured in the online journal *Analog Game Studies*. A full book on postcolonial studies of board games is the next logical step in this debate.

Putting board games in the focus of attention, we are engaging with the evolving field of board game studies. The "hegemony" of digital games is less overwhelming than it used to be in game research, just to mention the rise of the *Analog Game Studies* journal in 2014, and the opening of the leading journal *Game Studies* to nondigital games in 2017. Book-length board game studies from the last 10 years include Woods (2012), Booth (2015), Arnaudo (2018), Engelstein and Shalev (2020), and Calleja (2022). A notable most recent addition is Booth's *Board Games as Media* (2021): a comprehensive source for analysis of board games as representational media, and for ethnographic explorations of player audiences.

The first section in this chapter is essentially an annotated bibliography for postcolonial board game studies. The second section is an overview of chapters contributed to this volume. The third section is the editor's thoughts on the future developments of postcolonial board game studies, as can be predicted by current trends in both game studies and postcolonial studies.

The three sections may be labeled as the past, the present, and the future. This is not to suggest that previous research from Section 1 is somehow outdated as being relegated to "the past." Quite the opposite, previous research keeps informing our own and will inform the field for the years to come.

DOI: 10.4324/9781003356318-1

Postcolonial Game Studies: An Annotated Bibliography

Mukherjee and Hammar (2018), Introduction to the Special Issue on Postcolonial Perspectives in Game Studies

An introduction to the 2018 issue of the *Open Library of Humanities* 4(2), it includes a general layout of the landscape of postcolonial studies on games. It summarizes the then-existing research on postcolonial themes within game studies and also points to relevant publications selected from general postcolonial theory. The chapter also includes a brief overview of every other chapter in that collection. Taken together, Mukherjee and Hammar's introduction is an excellent overview of the state of postcolonial game studies by the year 2018, and a solid introduction to the key themes and issues within this field. Below, I will only summarize board games-centered papers from the 2018 collection, but all other papers are no less valuable for postcolonial reflection on games.

Borit, Borit and Olsen (2018), Representations of Colonialism in Three Popular, Modern Board Games: Puerto Rico, Struggle of Empires, and Archipelago

The title of this paper from the OLH 4(2) collection already tells us much about its purpose and scope. Borit et al. undertake a critical analysis of colonial(ist) representations in the three games, taking into account the game rules, visual design, physical components, and narrative themes. They are particularly interested in how the games construct the images of the colonizers and the colonized, and their mutual relations. The authors conclude that all the three games perpetuate the Eurocentic colonialist depictions of the colonized cultures. My personal highlights are Tables 1 and 2, which together build a strong framework for analysis of postcolonial representation in games. This is a useful contribution to the analytical toolkit of all game scholars in the field.

Bekesas, Berimbau, Mader, Pellerano and Riegel (2018), CosmoCult Card Game: A Methodological Tool to Understand the Hybrid and Peripheral Cultural Consumption of Young People

Another paper from OLH 4(2). The authors present the premises and results of research on how young people in Brazil construct representations of themselves and others (and The Other) in the context of cultural-aesthetic cosmopolitanism, as compared to the youth in several other countries. The project used the *CosmoCult* card game, developed as a tool for both research and education. The game was a storytelling engine, with cards functioning as prompts guiding the players' improvization with miscellaneous examples of popcultural tropes. Unlike most papers in postcolonial game studies, this paper does not analyze representations of colonialism in games – instead, it showcases the use of a nondigital game as a tool to study people and societies living in postcolonial conditions.

Harrer and Harviainen (2022), Where Are the White Perpetrators in All the Colonial Board Games? A Case Study on Afrikan tähti

From the perspective of Critical Whiteness Theory, Harrer, and Harviainen discuss the implied, though apparently absent, presence of white perpetrators in colonial-themed board games. Their case study is the 1951 Finnish game *Afrikan tähti* (also explored in our volume by Sivula and Suominen). Studying the design of maps, mechanics, and characters, they interpret the game as perpetuating white colonial whitewashing of European involvement. They also comment on the status of this game as a cherished cultural heritage in Finland, and its problematic connection to the view of Finnish exceptionalism.

Veracini (2013), Settlers of Catan

This short paper is a review of the game, interpreted here as a representation of settler colonialism. A leading theorist of settler colonialism, the author comes to the same conclusions that are later made by game scholars: about the problematic absence of indigenous people and about the suggested glorification of the colonial dream.

Wehrle (2016), Affective Networks at Play: Catan, COIN, and The Quiet Year

Wehrle compares game design in the three board games from the point of view of their affective possibilities – and affective consequences. The uncritical and apparently light-hearted approach to colonialism in *Catan* and the controversial anti-colonial insurgencies in COIN are here compared to "post-player affect" of the uniquely designed *The Quiet Year*. Wehrle demonstrates the three radically different games as generating different affects.

Robinson (2014), Orientalism and Abstraction in Eurogames

Robinson applies Said's notion of orientalism to the study of the 2009 board game *Vasco da Gama*, and draws some general conclusions on the genre of Eurogames. Robinson discusses how the game system represents early overseas colonialism as a highly abstracted simulation of seafaring and trading, leaving out the element of violence historically involved in these endeavors. The author critically comments on the apparent lack of political involvement in the European board game culture (in both the designer community and the market), and points to alternative strategies and potentials of using Eurostyle board games for politicized representations of colonial histories.

Foasberg (2016), The Problematic Pleasures of Productivity and Efficiency in Goa and Navegador

Foasberg continues Robinson's explorations of problematic abstractions and simplifications of colonialism. This she does on the example of two games, both of which put players in the shoes of European explorers and merchants – without including native populations in the picture. Foasberg identifies two models of represented colonial empires: provincial management in *Goa* and expansion of the empire in *Navegador*. Both, however, are focused on efficiency of their economies, erasing the history of colonial violence behind it.

Loring-Albright (2015), The First Nations of Catan: Practices in Critical Modification
This is not a research paper, but in my subjective judgment it fully deserves a place in the key bibliography informing postcolonial game studies. Loring-Albright is a game designer, who created *The First Nations of Catan* as an anti-colonial response to the award-winning *Settlers of Catan*. This essay reveals his intention, design choices at various stages of the project, and postmortem reflection on the final version. The main purpose was to recenter the colonial narrative of *Settlers* ... on the indigenous population, with game mechanics that would endow them not only with a greater agency but also with alternative strategies and tactics and winning conditions. This essay is a must-read for any scholar interested in anti-colonial game design as a critical practice.

LaPensée (2016), Indigenous Board Game Design in The Gift of Food
This paper is another self-reflective piece written by a designer involved in the creation of a decolonial board game. This game was designed in collaboration with Native American communities as a tool to express "cultural values including collaboration, stewardship, gratitude, and generosity." This is a collaborative game about a Native family sharing responsibilities and resources. LaPensée presents the gameplay and the ideas that informed the collaborative design. This is a must-read for anyone interested in designer board games as a means of expression of indigenous cultures.

Trammell (2016), How Dungeons&Dragons Appropriated the Orient
Trammell focuses on the *Oriental Adventures* expansion to D&D, exploring its sexist and racist stereotypes and general reductionist simplifications in the depiction of the Orient. While D&D is not strictly a board game (still, a tabletop one), Trammell's analysis of the orientalist assumptions of game mechanics seems highly applicable in board game contexts. So does his study of narrative and aesthetic tropes in and by themselves, as well as in their correlations with the said mechanics.

Mukherjee (2017), Videogames and Postcolonialism: Empire Plays Back
Although focused on video games, Mukherjee's book does directly refer to board games every now and then (pp. 12, 31–32, 94–95). More importantly, its Chapters 1 (Videogames and Postcolonialism: An Introduction) and 5 (Rethinking (Post)Colonialism in Videogames: Towards a Conclusion) constitute the most comprehensive theoretical proposal of marrying game studies with postcolonial studies, whose relevance is not limited to digital games only. Also Chapter 2, focused as they are on the study of spaces, characters,

and stories, may to a greater or lesser degree inform the study of the same aspects in colonialism-themed board games. (So can Mukherjee's 2018 further work in *Games and Culture*, titled "Playing Subaltern: Video Games and Postcolonialism.")

Booth (2021), Board Games as Media

Two chapters in Booth (2021) are of particular relevance to us. In Chapter 3 (Colonizing Mars: Ludic Discourse Analysis), Booth addresses the issue of colonialism on the example of science-fiction games about humans on Mars, nonetheless revealing the same earthly interplay of colonialism, capitalism, and colonial discourse. Booth's demonstration of LDA – Ludic Discourse Analysis – is an interesting methodological proposal for studies of postcolonial discourses in board games. (So does his model of Ludo-Textual Analysis from Chapter 1.) Booth's Chapter 8 (Cultural Studies of Games: Diversity and Inclusion in the Board Game Industry and Hobby) conducts an ethnographic study of the board game community and industry, including the issues of racism and colonialism. In particular, he discusses the case of *Scramble for Africa*, a board game project abandoned due to public outrage at its treatment of the theme. In general, colonialism and postcolonial theory do not occupy much space in the book, but many postcolonial studies of board games can utilize Booth's methods for textual and ethnographic analysis.

Arnaudo (2018), Storytelling in the Modern Board Game

This book, by contrast, does not mention colonialism or orientalism at all. It is entirely focused on storytelling and worldbuilding in tabletop games, including *Dungeons&Dragons*. Why did I place it among recommended bibliography for postcolonial board game studies? Because it is one of the most comprehensive applications of narrative theory to board games. Postcolonial game studies often explore the narrative layer of games, and this is where Arnaudo's toolbox comes in handy. This book may inform the study of (post) colonial narratives in games just as Booth (2021) can inform the study of (post)colonial discourses.

Chapters in This Volume

Chapters in this volume are destined to engage with the above bibliography in one way or another.

"Two, Three ... Many Vietnams." Anti-Colonial Struggle, Postcolonialism and Counterinsurgency in Historical Board Games

Giaime Alonge and Ricardo Fassone provide a chronological-historical context for the development of the COIN series of board wargames, which can be labeled as postcolonial. They trace the appearance and rising popularity of colonial settings as themes and asymmetric game mechanics in rulesets.

In particular, on the examples of games set in Vietnam, they explore asymmetry as a design choice which allows for the representation of differences between the colonized and the colonizers in goals, strategies, and resources. They also note the limitations of wargames in representing (post)colonial settings, especially those not related to warfare.

Design Elements in Postcolonial Commercial Historical Board Wargames

Maurice Suckling studies the design of several board games representing colonial or postcolonial situations, and proposes a combination of three factors as the desired design agenda for anti-colonial design. This may be seen as a response to the limitations identified by Alonge and Fassone. The three factors are: strategic-level agency assigned to colonized people, complex strategic-level asymmetries between the colonizers and the colonized, and their extension to conflict asymmetries on the operational and tactical levels. Suckling argues that these design elements exist in some renowned games that are critically acknowledged as successful in their anti-colonial agenda.

Colonialist and Anti-Colonialist Play in Spirit Island: A Ludo-Textual Analysis

Andrew Kemp–Wilcox applies Booth's method of ludo-textual analysis to the study of *Spirit Island.* The game was intentionally designed as anti-colonial, putting the player in control of native inhabitants invoking spirits to resist an external threat of colonization. Kemp–Wilcox reveals how the game, despite its overt anti-colonial message, is designed in a problematic way that seems to justify colonial tactics of confrontation – analogically to what Mukherjee (2017) observes about video games. Kemp–Wilcox concludes his chapter with recommendations on how game designers may avoid such pitfalls. His ideas resonate well with Suckling's.

Unearthing Ancient Roots? Recognizing and Redefining Mexican Identity through Board Games

Bastarrachea Magnani starts with an outline of Mexican cultural history and identity as a mix of pre-Hispanic cultures and the legacy of Spanish colonizers. He emphasizes the role of the *barocco* style in arts and culture as the best expression of Mexicanness, and traces its influence in traditional as well as recent Mexican board games. The chapter includes a detailed account of the board games market in Mexico, and calls for appreciation of board games as vehicles for expression of both Mexican themes and *barocco* aesthetics.

The Brazilian (Gamer) Culture through the Lenses of Nostalgia:
An Analysis of *Brazil: Imperial*

Thiago Falcão and Alexander Carneiro outline the Brazilian political and so-cial history, with particular focus on the nineteenth-century Imperial period as a special case of national nostalgia. They contextualize it in the recent Brazil-ian politics, marked by the rise of conservatism, and the influence of politics on society, including the gamer community. Their analysis moves from Bra-zilian video games to board games, and to their selected case study: the game *Brazil: Imperial*. Falcão and Carneiro identify ways in which the game glori-fies the imperial national past and ignores its dark sides, such as extermination and enslavement of native peoples.

Heritagisation and Heritage Conflict: The Finnish Afrikan Tähti
Board Game and Its Change to Contested Heritage, 1951–2021

Anna Sivula and Jaakko Suominen discuss the historically-changing public reception of the 1951 Finnish board game about colonial adventures in Africa, which has become a major commercial success. The authors take the heritage studies approach, viewing the game as a cultural heritage object, whose value has been constructed differently at different stages of history. In particular, they explore the clash between the heritage discourse constructing the game as a cherished family entertainment uniting generations of Finnish players – and the postcolonial discourse criticizing it for colonialism and racism. This chapter provides insight not only into the current state of the local heritage discourse(s) but also to its historical development.

No Meeples for "Scramble for Africa." Online Debates
on Playing Historical Trauma

Natàlia Lozano-Monterrubio, Juan Luis Gonzalo-Iglesia, and Núria Araüna-Baró explore the case of a (post)colonial game that was canceled before pub-lication. Unlike the previous chapters, the authors do not focus on the game project but on the related discussions on the online forums of the gamer com-munity. They explore how postcolonial theory and anti-colonial sentiments have entered the public debate, and they identify four main attitudes among the gamers. These are: ethical players, critical players, ludic players, and guilty-pleasure players. The ethical and critical attitudes, as authors conclude, may (and do) influence anti-colonial design in games such as *Spirit Island*.

Postcolonial Board Game Studies – Where Next?

After Booth (2021) and Arnaudo (2018), there should be no doubt that board games can be vehicles for meaningful discourses and narratives about the past – next to video games and tabletop role-playing games. After

Mukherjee (2017) and Mukherjee and Hammar (2018), the extension of postcolonial game studies to board games was already in progress, and its own book-length study was only to be expected. How can the field develop after this volume?

Undoubtedly, one trend will be thorough case studies of single games as ludo-textual representations of a (post)colonial situation, such as Kemp–Wilcox's analysis of *Spirit Island*. Alongside, there will be comparative studies of several games with related settings and/or rulesets, exemplified here by Suckling and by Alonge and Fassone. Single as well as comparative case studies are likely to focus on game design, representation and meaning-making, and they are likely to proceed from critical analysis to the formulation of design guidelines.

Another branch of research will focus on player communities – either on the English-speaking forums of the globalized gamer community and industry, or on local cultures in postcolonial countries. In this volume, Lozano-Monterrubio, Gonzalo-Iglesia, and Araüna-Baró represent the former, Falcão and Carneira and Bastarrachea Magnani the latter. The interest in regional game studies is clearly on the rise, and, as Liboriussen and Martin (2016) observe, it inevitably engages with postcolonial game studies. Speaking from the Polish perspective, I expect that regional studies of Central and Eastern European games will adopt the recent recognition of the intra-European colonization of Slavic and Baltic peoples (e.g., ECHOES project, Andersen, Knudsen & Kølvraa, 2018) as a valid subject of postcolonial studies.

Postcolonial past and present can also be approached from the angle of heritage studies. Colonialism-themed games as representations of the past – and even more so their players as audiences – are influenced by existing heritage narratives and discourses. Many issues discussed in postcolonial theory can be explored from the angle of heritage studies: Smith's (2006) authorized heritage discourse, Harvey's (2001) heritageization, Tunbridge and Ashworth's (1996) dissonance, or Harrison's (2013) dialogism. Elsewhere, I have argued for a heritage studies approach to historical nondigital role-playing (Mochocki, 2021a) and historical video games (Mochocki, 2021b). In this volume, the lens of heritage is successfully employed in the study of a board game by Sivula and Suominen. Yet another form of games-as-heritage are traditional board games viewed as local (sometimes – indigenous) cultural heritage, here explored by Bastarrachea Magnani.

The most profound insight I see in postcolonial game studies is the precise identification of the gap between intent and execution in games that aim to be anti-colonial, but design systems which simply empower the once-colonized with the means to become a superior colonizer, "effectively tying into the logic that they seek to overturn" (Mukherjee, 2018, p. 14). Kemp–Wilcox in this volume shows this on the example of *Spirit Island*. I take the intent-execution gap as a lesson not only for game design but also for postcolonial theory-crafting in the Western academia. Isn't it itself at risk of becoming a new hegemonic discourse that authorizes itself globally as "universal truths" defined by West-dominated academic power structures? This is a thought I will develop another time.

All these trends and foci have predecessors before this volume, as can be seen in the annotated bibliography above. We all stand on the shoulders of giants – and lend our shoulders to those that come after us.

References

Andersen, Casper, Britta Timm Knudsen, and Christoffer Kølvraa, eds. 2018. *ECHOES. European Colonial Heritage Modalities in Entangled Cities. Methodological Toolkit.* Aarhus: Aarhus University.

Arnaudo, Marco. 2018. *Storytelling in the Modern Board Game: Narrative Trends from the Late 1960s to Today. Studies in Gaming.* Jefferson, NC: McFarland & Company, Inc., Publishers.

Bekesas, Wilson Roberto, Mauro Berimbau, Renato Vercesi Mader, Joana Pellerano, and Viviane Riegel. 2018. 'CosmoCult Card Game: A Methodological Tool to Understand the Hybrid and Peripheral Cultural Consumption of Young People'. *Open Library of Humanities* 4 (1): 21. https://doi.org/10.16995/olh.167

Booth, Paul. 2015. *Game Play: Paratextuality in Contemporary Board Games.* New York, NY: Bloomsbury Academic.

Booth, Paul. 2021. *Board Games as Media.* New York, NY: Bloomsbury Academic.

Borit, Cornel, Melania Borit, and Petter Olsen. 2018. 'Representations of Colonialism in Three Popular, Modern Board Games: Puerto Rico, Struggle of Empires, and Archipelago'. *Open Library of Humanities* 4 (1): 17. https://doi.org/10.16995/olh.211

Calleja, Gordon. 2022. *Unboxed: Board Game Experience and Design.* Cambridge, MA: The MIT Press.

Engelstein, Geoffrey, and Isaac Shalev. 2020. *Building Blocks of Tabletop Game Design: An Encyclopedia of Mechanisms.* Boca Raton, FL: Taylor & Francis.

Foasberg, Nancy. 2016. 'The Problematic Pleasures of Productivity and Efficiency in Goa and Navegador'. *Analog Game Studies* III (I). https://analoggamestudies. org/2016/01/the-problematic-pleasures-of-productivity-and-efficiency-in-goa-and-navegador/

Harrer, Sabine, and J. Tuomas Harviainen. 2022. 'Where Are the White Perpetrators in All the Colonial Board Games? A Case Study on Afrikan Tähti'. In *Representing Conflicts in Games*, by Jonas Linderoth, Björn Sjöblom, and Anders Frank, 171–87. London: Routledge. https://doi.org/10.4324/9781003297406-14

Harrison, Rodney. 2013. *Heritage: Critical Approaches.* Milton Park, Abingdon, New York: Routledge.

LaPensée, Elizabeth. 2016. 'Indigenous Board Game Design in The Gift of Food'. *Analog Game Studies* III (II). https://analoggamestudies.org/2016/03/indigenous-board-game-design-in-the-gift-of-food/

Liboriussen, Bjarke, and Paul Martin. 2016. 'Regional Game Studies'. *Game Studies* 16 (1). http://gamestudies.org/1601/articles/liboriussen

Loring-Albright, Greg. 2015. 'The First Nations of Catan: Practices in Critical Modification'. *Analog Game Studies* II (VII). https://analoggamestudies.org/2015/ 11/the-first-nations-of-catan-practices-in-critical-modification/

Mochocki, Michał. 2021a. *Role-Play as a Heritage Practice: Historical LARP, Table-top RPG and Reenactment*. Abingdon, Oxon, New York, NY: Routledge.

Mochocki, Michał. 2021b. 'Heritage Sites and Video Games: Questions of Authenticity and Immersion'. *Games and Culture* 16 (8): 951–77. https://doi.org/10.1177/15554120211005369

Mukherjee, Souvik. 2017. *Videogames and Post-Colonialism: Empire Plays Back*. Palgrave Pivot. Cham: Palgrave Macmillian.

Mukherjee, Souvik. 2018. 'Playing Subaltern: Video Games and Postcolonialism'. *Games and Culture* 13 (5): 504–20. https://doi.org/10.1177/1555412015627258

Mukherjee, Souvik, and Emil Lundedal Hammar. 2018. 'Introduction to the Special Issue on Postcolonial Perspectives in Game Studies', November. https://doi.org/10.16995/olh.309

Robinson, Will. 2014. 'Orientalism and Abstraction in Eurogames'. *Analog Game Studies* I (V). https://analoggamestudies.org/2014/12/orientalism-and-abstraction-in-eurogames/

Smith, Laurajane. 2006. *Uses of Heritage*. London, New York: Routledge, Taylor & Francis Group.

Trammell, Aaron. 2016. 'How *Dungeons&Dragons* Appropriated the Orient'. *Analog Game Studies* III (I). https://analoggamestudies.org/2016/01/how-dungeons-dragons-appropriated-the-orient/

Tunbridge, J. E., and G. J. Ashworth. 1996. *Dissonant Heritage: The Management of the Past as a Resource in Conflict*. Chichester, NY: J. Wiley.

Veracini, Lorenzo. 2013. 'Settlers of Catan'. *Settler Colonial Studies* 3 (1): 131–33. https://doi.org/10.1080/18380743.2013.761941

Wehrle, Cole. 2016. 'Affective Networks at Play: Catan, COIN, and The Quiet Year'. *Analog Game Studies* III (III). https://analoggamestudies.org/2016/05/affective-networks-at-play-catan-coin-and-the-quiet-year/

Woods, Stewart. 2012. *Eurogames: The Design, Culture and Play of Modern European Board Games*. Jefferson, NC: McFarland & Co.

2 "Two, Three … Many Vietnams"

Anti-Colonial Struggle, Postcolonialism, and Counterinsurgency in Historical Board Games

Giaime Alonge

Riccardo Fassone[1]

Introduction

Wargames, and historically themed boardgames more generally, deal in abstractions. They rely on a peculiar form of digitization: military campaigns turned into numbers, with units on the battlefield eliminated or pronounced victorious on the basis of (often byzantine) interactions between their numeric values and dice rolls. Wargames have traditionally avoided simulating all the non-military components of warfare, such as political reasons behind a war or civilians' involvement (usually as victims). Furthermore, wargames have typically sought to simulate scenarios, campaigns and battles considered historically or politically relevant from a Western standpoint. In other words, wargames seem to contribute, albeit marginally, to a historical project that historian Carlo Ginzburg describes as "wanting to know only about 'the great deeds of Kings'" (1980, 2).

As a hobby, wargaming was born in the fifties in the United States and reached its apex in the seventies and early eighties. During this so-called "golden age", wargames almost entirely ignored anti-colonial struggle as a theme. In the last 20 years, things have dramatically changed, with many games – the so-called COIN series (COIN standing for COunterINsurgency) – simulating insurrection, guerilla and unconventional warfare. In our chapter (which is somehow a "prequel" to Maurice Suckling's), we analyze the almost total absence – along with a relevant exception – of anti-colonial campaigns in wargames from the seventies and eighties, and the emergence of these topics in connection with a new kind of gameplay centered on cards. We will highlight innovations – both ludic and political – but also similarities between traditional hex-and-counter wargames and card-driven COIN games.

DOI: 10.4324/9781003356318-2

This chapter will thus attempt at answering two questions: (1) What are the modes of engagement of "traditional" wargames with anti- or postcolonial scenarios? and (2) in which terms can contemporary wargames such as COIN be described as postcolonial?

Clarifications on Semantics

This chapter is concerned with objects that we define as "postcolonial wargames". This shorthand definition allows us to group under one convenient label a number of games that are rather disparate and disparately implicated in postcolonialism as a historical state of affairs, a theoretical disposition, and/or a political stance. For this reason, our definition of wargames is relatively loose. We apply this label to games that conform to the now-crystalised look and feel of the golden age of wargaming: a hexagonal grid superimposed over a map of a real location; counters representing units on the battlefield with the ability to move around following specific rules; battles fought by comparing numeric factors. We also use the term to describe games that introduced significant alterations to the abovementioned model. These games introduced ways of simulating the political or diplomatic implications of the players' decisions, which would, in turn, allow designers to depict less battle-focused scenarios and situations.

The notion of postcolonialism, and the adjective "postcolonial", describe the critical analysis of the effects, implications, and ramifications of the historical processes of imperialism and colonisation. While the term "postcolonialism" seems to imply a temporal chain of events – "post-" being that which comes after something – it should be said that, as noted by Mukherjee (2017, loc. 112), "[t]he term itself does not simply mean "*after* colonialism", the end of colonialism, or even solely address the scenarios in the formerly colonized countries *after* their independence". Following Mukherjee's broad understanding of the postcolonial, we define postcolonial wargames as those that engage with one or more of the following:

1   the historical process of decolonisation, that is the acquisition, albeit partial, of political independence of formerly colonised territories;
2   the military, economic, and political processes that can be observed in formerly colonised territories, such as the establishment of new forms of governance, the emergence of indigenous social actors, etc.;
3   the political implications and effects of a postcolonial ideological stance, that is, according to Loomba (1998, 12), "the contestation of colonial domination and the legacies of colonialism";
4   the repercussions of colonial history in the present, such as the influence of anti-colonial movements in contemporary anti-imperialist struggles, and the experiences of subjects affected by postcolonial diasporas.

Postcolonial wargames, we claim, are boardgames that, while falling within the lineage of classic wargaming, acknowledge, and usually enter in some form of relation with, the ramified implications and legacies of colonialism, either by simply deciding to simulate colonial confrontations (such as the battle of Dien Bien Phu), or by engaging with the power dynamics that emerge in formerly colonised territories.

Playing Anti-Colonial Insurgency during Wargame's Golden Age

From its very beginning in the fifties to its heyday in the seventies and early eighties, hobby board wargames had no interest in guerrilla actions, low-intensity warfare, and anti-colonial struggle, even if international politics in the sixties and seventies was largely dominated by this kind of confrontations. Games produced by Avalon Hill and SPI – just to mention the two main publishers of the time – were mostly focused on conventional warfare, especially from the Nineteenth century and the first part of the Twentieth. As Richard Barbrook points out in *Class Wargames: Ludic Subversion against Spectacular Capitalism*, even Situationist thinker Guy Debord, when engaged in designing a strategy game, *Le Jeu de la Guerre*, in 1965 (published as a prototype in 1977, and then as a book in 1987), created a game modelling a Napoleonic era-like battle, ignoring "the anti-imperialist struggles of his own times" (Barbrook, 2014, 282), even though – as another Debord's scholar, Emmanuel Guy, points out – the Algerian War and its mediatisation played a relevant role in Debord's thinking (see Guy, 2020, 45–46).

While the question Barbrook poses – why did Debord ignore the anti-colonial struggles of his time? – is stimulating, his answer is not really convincing. Barbrook's thesis is that Debord aimed at "reappropriating" the ideas of military thinker Carl von Clausewitz, hijacked by "bad guys" of different ideological lineage: American imperialists on the one hand, and Stalinists on the other (Barbrook, 2014, 290–291). Many great Communist leaders, from Lenin to Tito and Mao, were von Clausewitz's avid readers, and von Clausewitz's doctrines were part of several Party schools' curricula (see NLR Editors, 1968; Derbent, 2006).[2] From a Marxist perspective, of course, the more interesting part of von Clausewitz's magnus opus is the chapter about *Volksbewaffnung*, "the people in arms" (see von Clausewitz, 1984, 479–483). The notion of *Volksbewaffnung* represents only a small part of von Clausewitz complex doctrine, which is largely focused on professional armies and the "decisive" battles they fight. A decisive battle (*Entscheidungsschlacht*) is a battle aimed at destroying enemy forces, which, according to von Clausewitz, is the first goal of any commander. This kind of military encounter represents the main subject of hobby wargames. If Debord, for his game, modelled a Napoleonic era-like battle is simply because that was the dominant pattern in wargame design.³ In its heyday, wargames not only largely ignored low-intensity warfare and anti-colonial struggle, but more generally any warfare outside the *Entscheidungsschlacht* pattern. Along with anti-colonial guerrilla, also World War One trench warfare – where manoeuvre was almost impossible and battles hardly decisive – was largely ignored. It is no accident that the only episode in the history of the struggle for decolonisation that is depicted in several wargames from the seventies and early eighties is the battle of Dien Bien Phu, where a Vietnamese army crushed the finest units of the French army, putting an end to the French colonial rule in South-East Asia.

The battle of Dien Bien Phu, fought between March 13 and May 7, 1954, is a quintessential decisive battle, very similar, in its nature and outcome, to the great battles of World War Two, such as El Alamein or Stalingrad. As Christopher Goscha notes in his *The Road to Dien Bien Phu* (2022), this battle represents a real *unicum* in the history of anti-colonial struggle. Normally, anti-imperialist movements, in what was once known as the Third World, did not possess enough economic resources nor professional expertise to organise a conventional army able to engage a Western army in an open-field confrontation. In the global South, normally triumph against government/imperialist forces depended – and still depends – on asymmetrical warfare: subversion, terrorism, guerrilla. On the contrary, in the valley of Dien Bien Phu, at the end of the Indochina War, the Vietnamese leadership – also thanks to Chinese assistance – was able to put on the ground an army of 51.000 soldiers, organised into four infantry divisions, with massive artillery support. It is something others, such as the Algerian *Front de libération nationale*, tried to replicate, but never could.

The games on the battle of Dien Bien Phu we referred to were released between 1977 and 1980, respectively in Sweden, the United States and France. The American game is called *Citadel: The Battle of Dien Bien Phu* (GDW, 1977) and was published by Game Designer's Workshop, a very active company at the time, famous for making so-called monster games: highly time-consuming games with very large maps and thousands of counters. *Citadel* is not exactly a monster game, because it has "only" 320 counters representing military units, plus 168 markers, but the battle is still simulated with remarkable granularity. The scale is quite low, with each hexagon covering 200 yards from side to side, and counters representing quite small units, from infantry companies of about 100 men to a single tank (there were just ten at Dien Bien Phu). The rules governing the game are not particularly difficult, but they need quite a slow and tiring execution, with an elaborate – if brilliant – system of movement under artillery fire. The French game, *Diên Biên Phu. La bataille decisive de la guerre d'Indochine* (Jeux Descartes, 1980) is simpler and shorter than *Citadel*, but belongs to the same category of hex-and-counter wargames. We were not able to find a copy of the Swedish game (Swedish Game

Production, 1977) to play, but examining the images found online, it is evident this is another hex-and-counter simulation.

These kinds of games tend to focus exclusively on the military dimension. Politics and ideology play no explicit role in the gameplay, even if a battle such as Dien Bien Phu was partially fought during a peace conference. In *Citadel*, the only political reference is a rule about the possibility that civilian pilots, hired by the French air force to fly transport planes, go on strike, reducing supplies for the besieged garrison. The French game, probably because the designer had a deeper connection to that story, does offer a political angle. Here, reinforcements partially depend on the disposition of the French government.[4] If the troops on the ground get good scores in body count, the politicians are pleased and send more men and materials, in order to negotiate in Geneva from a stronger position. It is quite telling that only the French player has a political phase in the turn sequence. The Vietnamese side, labelled as "communist" in the rulebook, is presented as having no inner tensions. In the Western mental framework of the Cold War, the communist bloc is a bloc by definition – no nuances. While France has a political debate on supporting the war in Asia, the Vietnamese are presented as a monolith, even if – as Goscha shows in his book – the Vietnamese anti-imperialist front had quite a nuanced political spectrum, from middle-class nationalists to Marxists. As Paul Booth (2021) has shown, board games, as any other cultural artefact, may express a political position. *Diên Biên Phu*'s rulebook is clearly infused with colonial nostalgia (Indochina is called "one of our oldest colonies"), and the French army is depicted as bravely fighting, in spite of tricky politicians and a distracted public opinion. What is totally lacking is the political nature of the anti-colonial struggle.

Of course, one could argue that a game simulating a single battle cannot model the political dimension because there is none. Battles are about fighting. If there is a political dimension in the anti-colonialist struggle in Indochina, it is *before* Dien Bien Phun, when the Vietnamese leadership waged a prolonged guerrilla warfare and at the same time built a field army. On this topic, there is a fourth game from wargame's "golden age". It is deceptively titled *Dien Bien Phu* (Flying Buffalo, 1977), because it actually simulates the entire Indochina war and not just its final battle, as its subtitle explains: *Strategic Game of Indochina 1950–55*. This game is interesting because, albeit dealing with insurrection, it models it without any reference to politics or unconventional warfare. The counters on the map represent both regular and irregular units, but there is no substantial difference in the way they fight.

As Jason Matthews (2021) argues, traditional hex-and-counter wargames tend to offer a quantitative approach to political problems, translating ideological and cultural confrontations to numerical factors, to write on counters or register on a track. We find this kind of approach even in a game such as *South Africa: The Death of Colonialism*, an SPI production from 1977, that imagined a possible collapse of the apartheid regime. The game tries to account for the economic and political dimension of the conflict between black insurgents and the white government, but models these problems in a pure mathematical form, and centres its main focus on quintessential hex-and-counter gameplay, with the blacks attacking government forces with regular troops (infantry and armour battalions, and even airplanes) in an open-field confrontation. Also the victory conditions – which angered some members of the South Africa's leadership of the time, because the game asserted that the apartheid system could not last forever (see Palmer, 1980, 47) – are based on conventional warfare logic, with the black player winning by controlling a certain number of cities and towns, just like in a game about Operation Barbarossa.

While the wargame industry, in its heyday, systematically ignored the peculiarities of insurgency and unconventional warfare, professional wargame designers – i.e. designers working for governmental agencies – tried to simulate the specificity of those conflicts. In 1965, at the beginning of the Vietnam war, the Pentagon commissioned a "COIN game". It was made by ABT Associates Inc., a newly created think tank from Cambridge, Massachusetts. The report produced by ABT is a thick text of more than 200 pages, titled "Counter-Insurgency Game Design: Feasibility and Evaluation Study", and can be found on the Internet Archive. It has almost no explicit reference to Vietnam (beside a quotation from a Viet Cong directive at page B-31), but it is self-evident that the insurrection in Southeast Asia is the context. The text presents the game mechanics and describes a series of games played over several months. This is an analogue game, but with a possible computer expansion. It is not a wargame, but a roleplaying game, conceived for a large number of players. There are three different factions – insurgents, who must take over villages and get the local population's loyalty; government forces, who must do the same; and the villagers, whose only goal is survival. The text is quite blunt about the nature of this kind of warfare, discussing the recurse to abduction and simulated murder. Of course, the use of such a lexicon would have been inconceivable in a commercial product, at least in the sixties and seventies. But in order to produce a COIN game, the wargame industry had not only to wait for a cultural change in society, with players eager to play a game about insurrection and terrorism. It also had to develop new game mechanics, more apt than hex and counters at simulating this kind of conflicts.

COIN Games as Postcolonial Wargames

Starting with the early eighties, with the rise of digital games, "traditional" wargaming began to lose steam. This period "increasingly saw players pursuing the hobby in digital form" (Woods, 2012, 24). It is perhaps not an accident then that, in the attempt to diversify their catalogue, prominent wargame publishers started releasing games that challenged some of the established assumptions. It is the case, for example of *Guerrilla* (Avalon

Hill, 1994), a card game with no board, that tasks players with conducting guerrilla campaigns in an unspecified (but clearly coded as Mesoamerican or Latin-American) location. The game is largely played by comparing numeric values on sets of cards that act as skirmishing factions, but players are also required to engage in trading negotiations for cards. While apparently prosaic, this mechanic seems to hint at an interest in mitigating the traditionally stiff and math-driven procedures of wargames with more idiosyncratic rules. As we will discuss when analysing COIN games, encouraging players to engage in negotiations or use deceptive strategies is one of the most recurrent design features in games modelling non-conventional warfare. Despite a suggestive title and a visual identity that hints at existing guerrilla formations such as the Nicaraguan Contras or the Colombian FARC, the game never really addresses any specific historical or political scenarios. The warring factions are described as "pro-Government" and "pro-Rebels" with very little indication of who the rebels are and what they are rebelling against. This restraint in offering historical detail is particularly odd, considering the quasi-fetishist attitude that wargame designers and publishers held towards historical verisimilitude. A similar strategy can be observed in the video game *Tropico* (PopTop Software, 2001), which casts the player in the role of a somewhat benevolent Latin-American dictator, whose task is to keep the country's economy afloat. No geographical or historical details are provided, an obfuscation that, coupled with the relatively straightforward mechanics that ask players to extract and manage resources in a way similar to other games of the genre, can be seen as an attempt to normalise the political implications of US intervention in Mesoamerican and Latin-American regime changes. A proceduralist analysis of the game, conducted by Magnet (2006, 143), concludes that *Tropico*'s jovial aesthetics and familiar rules are extremely effective "in concealing the underlying assumptions of the game, many of which are intimately tied to ideas about U.S. imperialist expansion, [to the point] that it could posited as a useful education tool."[5] While *Guerrilla* is certainly less sophisticated in its simulation of the implications of American imperialism, the removal of all explicit references to historical facts and political positions can be interpreted as a sign of the wariness of designers and publishers towards the simulation of non-canonical wargame scenarios.

This reluctance was definitively overcome in 2012, when the then-largest wargame publisher globally, GMT, published *Andean Abyss*, a card-driven historical simulation of the political and military tensions in 1990s Colombia. *Andean Abyss* marked a significant departure from the canon for several reasons. The use of cards, as in *Guerrilla*, is consistent with a trend emerging in the 1990s and early 2000s, with historical games such as *We the People* (Avalon Hill, 1993) and *Twilight Struggle* (GMT, 2005) using a deck of cards to introduce chance and variety as main drivers of players' strategy. As noted earlier, in traditional wargaming dice were the main vessel for chance, used as modifiers to the units' strength in battle. Cards, on the other hand, are generally used to implement a degree of unforeseeability, which the players need to mitigate strategically.[6] According to Wehrle (2016), by forcing players to form unstable and temporary alliances, and thus rely on each other, these mechanics, at least in certain circumstances, elicit a significantly different affective approach than more traditional wargaming. A more radical departure from the conventions is that *Andean Abyss* is for 1 to 4 players. Generally, wargames simulated bipolar confrontations of two armies,[7] but Ruhnke's game has four competing factions (the Government, the Marxist group FARC, the paramilitary formation AUC, and the drug-trafficking cartel) with significant differences in objectives and means. *Andean Abyss* was the first game released under the COIN label, a series published by GMT and curated by Volko Ruhnke, "presenting guerrilla warfare, asymmetric warfare, and COunterINsurgencies around the world – in both historical and contemporary conflicts" (GMT, no date).[8] The games in the series all employ a common game system, with single mechanics tweaked to suit the simulative requirements of different scenarios. COIN is generally used in military jargon to describe situations in which an institutional faction (e.g. a government, an occupying force, etc.) faces resistance from local insurgent factions that generally employ non-conventional warfare strategies such as guerrilla or terrorism. The term was popularised by David Galula (1964), who had served in the French-Algerian war and had observed interactions between the French and the local population.

Ten years after *Andean Abyss*, the COIN series now features ten entries and has spawned several apocryphal games who use the COIN game system despite not being published by GMT or curated by Ruhnke. The ten official COIN games model conflicts such as the Cuban revolution, the Vietnam war, and the Gallic revolt against Ceasar. All COIN games simulate scenarios in which different factions battle for possession of a territory, albeit with a significant variety in scale, and do so by tasking players with diplomatic, economic, and military actions. Implicit in the notion of "asymmetric warfare" is the fact that different factions have different capabilities and resources, with governmental factions generally being more affluent in resources, and insurgent ones having the advantage of rapidity and secretiveness. Despite these general premises, not all games deal with scenarios that can be defined as postcolonial in one of the senses articulated earlier in the chapter. While *Gandhi: The Decolonization of British India, 1917–1947* (GMT, 2019) explicitly tackles questions of postcolonial struggle and the aftermath of British imperialism, a game like *All Bridges Burning: Red Revolt and White Guard in Finland, 1917–1918* (GMT, 2020) deals with a series of historical events – the struggle for independence and the civil war in Finland in the shadow of the Russian revolution – that generally fall outside the scope of postcolonial theory and historiography. In this light, COIN games seem to adopt notions such as "asymmetric" and "guerrilla" warfare as umbrella terms for very different scenarios and frame a postcolonial state of affairs as one of many factors contributing to asymmetric confrontations.

To explore how postcolonial themes and situations are simulated in COIN games, we chose *Colonial Twilight: The French-Algerian War, 1954–62* (GMT, 2017), designed by Brian Train, that aims at offering a political, diplomatic and military overview of the war for the independence of Algeria. Atypically for the COIN series, *Colonial Twilight* is for two players, one playing as the French colonial forces (comprising the French army and police, along with their auxiliary Algerian soldiers and policemen), the other as the FLN. Despite being a two-player game, *Colonial Twilight* retains some of the uncertainty in alliances that are trademark of the COIN series, as some of the French pieces (markedly Algerian army and police forces) can be turned into FLN (Front de libération nationale) pieces by an action called "Subversion". Except for this simulation of the desertion of Algerian forces,[9] the game is structured as a bipolar confrontation between a militarily superior occupying force and an insurgent force that has greater mobility and more stable support from the local population. While the map of the game represents Algeria, the "France Track" abstracts the support to the war effort from the French public opinion; this track can be influenced either by the Algerian player, who can spend resources to gain sympathy from Algerian expatriates living in France, or by the amount of French casualties, which will inevitably lower the commitment of the French population. As in all other COIN games, the cards represent a mixture of historical events (e.g. "Peace of the Brave", which explicitly cites de Gaulle's proposed amnesty for FLN prisoners, called "paix des braves"), historical figures (e.g. "Taleb the Bomb-maker", based on the life of the terrorist Abderrahmane Taleb), and general processes and dynamics that are considered influential in the outcome of the war (e.g. "Balky Conscripts", representing the reluctance of French conscripts to fight in Algeria).

One notable characteristic of the selection of characters, events, and processes – very telling of the approach to postcolonialism – is the absence of the local population except as a recipient of the effects of certain events. The game map informs players of the population of each sector, using numbers from 0, for mostly deserted or mountainous areas, to 3 for large cities such as Algiers. This abstraction of the population as mere numerical value effectively turns civilians into an asset that can be mobilised by the two players. The French player is allowed to relocate civilians from an area (an operation called Resettlement) in order to weaken the guerrilla bands; the FLN player can recruit insurgents in more densely populated areas and generate opposition to the French government in the local population. As a result of this abstraction, for both players, the local population has value only as a currency for opportunistic moves. This dynamic is described by scholars of postcolonialism and nationalism such as Chatterjee (1993) as one of the potential aftermaths of colonialism, one in which anti-colonial forces may in fact seek to establish nationalist forms of governance that may end up being as despotic to civilians as those of the former colonists.

It is interesting to notice that such erasure of the civilian population as a political actor is performed in a game set during the French-Algerian war, a conflict heavily featured in the work of psychiatrist and activist Frantz Fanon. Some of his most cited works (e.g. 1967, 2008) on the French-Algerian war can be considered a major touchstone in postcolonial critique. More specifically, as noted by Sonnleitner (1987), Fanon, an unorthodox Marxist, argued for a radical decentralisation of the postcolonial struggle, since "only violent action on the part of the native would reveal the existence of the underlying violence of capitalist colonial exploitation" (292). Train's game may be said to deliberately steer clear of this intellectual tradition, a choice reinforced by the fact that *Colonial Twilight*'s bibliographic sources are comprised almost completely of historical or military accounts of the war.[10]

Despite all the differences from traditional hex-and-counter wargames, COIN games tend to adhere to a similar quantitative approach, and favour military and political actors. If the Pentagon COIN game from 1964 (see previous section) represented the villagers as an active participant in diplomacy, it is precisely because that was more a roleplaying game than a wargame.

It may be said that consistently with COIN's idea of multi-factional struggle over a territory, the deck of cards of *Colonial Twilight* establishes the game as a text that understands the process of decolonisation of Algeria as one that "does not apply to those at the bottom end of this hierarchy [i.e. the social and economic hierarchy], who are still "at the far economic margins of the nation-state" so that nothing is "post about their colonization" (Loomba, 1998, 9). This interest in the power struggle between colonisers and a somewhat institutional insurrectional force such as the FLN is compounded by Train's design notes (2017), where he claims, in tune with Galula's theory of counterinsurgency, that one should remember that political change in colonised territories is always pursued and eventually obtained by a minority, while a large majority of the local population is essentially armless and politically volatile. This is cleverly reflected in the rules that decouple the act of establishing control over a territory (either for the FLN or the French) from that of gaining the conditional support of the population. While both actions are useful, winning conditions are ultimately dictated by territorial dominance. Train's game does not aim at representing the standpoint of the colonised population. It can be described as postcolonial in the sense that it allows players to play out the power struggle that ensues from (i.e. "after") colonialism. It represents postcolonialism not as the emotional, political, social struggle of the postcolonial subject, but rather as the interplay of different actors in a postcolonial landscape. *Colonial Twilight* does not engage in representing the vicissitudes of the civilian population, except for a very telling case. The card "Atrocities and reprisals", built upon the mechanic of terrorism found in the game, represents what Train describes as follows:

> Both sides were responsible for savage and grotesque atrocities during the war, and one violent incident would often spark a cycle of vicious action and reaction. While there were FLN-sponsored terrorist incidents in France, it was the ordinary people of Algeria (white, Arab and native) who paid disproportionately with their lives and limbs. As with most wars of the 20th century, the great majority of casualties in the war were civilian.
>
> (2017, 18)

Train's note on the meaning and implications is telling in two regards. On the one hand, it implicitly acknowledges the shortcomings of simulative games (both traditional wargames and contemporary COIN games) in accounting for the suffering of civilians. On the other hand, it frames the atrocities of the French-Algerian war as "spark[ing] a cycle of vicious action and reaction", thus alluding to the "gamey" dynamic of back-and-forth terrorist coups that the rules of *Colonial Twilight* implicitly elicit. This abstraction of terrorism as a spiral in which two actors engage in increasingly brutal acts more or less explicitly erases the asymmetries, both in their goals and means, between the actors. This design choice can be interpreted in the light of a theory of postcolonial terrorism that, once more, pictures the struggle over Algeria as aimed at establishing dominance over a nation-state, a depiction of postcolonialism that Parashar (2018) describes as postcolonial nationalism, a dynamic that was only one, albeit dominant, of several political doctrines adopted by the insurgents (Fanon 1967). Train's reflection reads as the realisation that making boardgames necessarily implies a process of quantification and proceduralisation of real-life dynamics.

Conclusions

In recent years, wargames and, more generally, historical simulations, have started to tackle less traditional subjects, and have developed an interest in the representation of asymmetric and, more specifically, postcolonial conflicts. Games such as the GMT's COIN series have expanded the reach of historical simulations beyond the technicalities of conventional warfare towards more nuanced representations of history. Nevertheless, the genealogy of wargaming can be observed in games such as *Colonial Twilight*, which simulate decolonisation and postcolonial scenarios by mitigating the highly abstracted and mathematically structured rulesets of wargames through the use of asymmetric capabilities and expressive procedures. These may not be the "truly" postcolonial games described, for example, by LaPensée (2016), but their existence as one of the facets of wargaming speaks to the growing relevance of games to the formation of the postcolonial discourse in Western media. COIN games introduced new actors and themes, such as insurgents and guerrillas, into games that had for a long time simulated only conventional warfare. On the other hand, COIN games, while reinventing the basics of gameplay (especially through a card deck), continue the tradition of hex-and-counter wargame, as they still focus on the dialectics between political-military actors, more or less ignoring the civil society. This dialectics – often involving four players – can be more complex than the bipolar logic of the hex and counter, but the playable factions are still power groups (government, political opposition, criminal organisations). From this perspective, COIN games lucidly simulate the tragic outcomes of anti-colonial struggle in many countries, which, notwithstanding the high hopes of well-intentioned militants and thinkers such as Frantz Fanon, passed from colonial rule to brutal dictatorships of former rebels turned government.

Notes

1 This chapter should be considered a result of teamwork, with all paragraphs discussed and edited by both authors. Nevertheless, Alonge wrote the section on hex-and-counter wargames, and Fassone wrote the section titled "Clarification on Semantics" and the section on COIN games.

2 On Clausewitz's connection with Marxism – through Hegel – see André Glucksman's (1967) *Le discours de la guerre*.

3 On Debord's knowledge of hobby wargames of his times, see Guy (2020, 144–145, 173).

4 Nevertheless, the American designer of *Citadel*, in the notes at the end of the rulebook, refers to his "national" connection to that story, when he writes that Dien Bien Phu is "linked to a certain extent to our own Vietnamese adventure". This game was published just two years after the fall of Saigon. The author also mentions that, at the time, neither the French nor the American war in Southeast Asia experienced "dazzling acceptance by the gaming public".

5 While, to our knowledge, this is the first attempt at discussing postcolonialism in analogue historical simulations, video game studies have a tradition of dealing with such themes. On the colonialist implications of the 4X (eXplore, eXpand, eXploit, eXterminate) genre, see Ford (2016). Mukherjee (2018), offers an analysis of the representation of the postcolonial subject in video games. A general overview of the methods and tools developed by video game studies to discuss postcolonial issues can be found in Mukherjee and Hammar (2018).

6 In COIN and other similar card-driven games, cards can be said to reposition chance in the chain of events forming a turn. While in more traditional wargames dice are rolled after a player has committed to attacking, in card-driven games cards represent preconditions for action. Such a distinction is analysed by game designer Noel Llopis (2013) in a blog post in which he describes these two conditions as "post-luck" and "pre-luck".

7 There are exceptions to this rule, a notable one being *Rise and Decline of the Third Reich* (Avalon Hill, 1974), which could be played by two players – one playing as the Axis and the other as the Allies – or by a variable number of players, up to six, controlling the different powers, each one with their own victory objectives.

8 See also Train and Ruhnke (2016).
9 According to Gortzak (2009), the Algerian forces fighting for the French saw a relatively small desertion rate. It should be noted that it is common for COIN and COIN-like games to represent military units in a more abstract and often less numerically precise way when compared to hex-and-counter wargames.
10 Despite this simulative focus, Train's game cannot be said to be completely impermeable to the cultural dimension of the conflict. One of the most notable cards in the deck is titled *Jean-Paul Sartre*, the French intellectual who vocally opposed the war. The card may have different effects depending on the player who activates it, but – as the flavor text reads – "Either way, he and Albert Camus are not friends anymore."

References – books and papers

ABT Associates Inc., *Counter-Insurgency Game Design: Feasibility and Evaluation Study*. Cambridge, MA: ABT Associates Inc., 1965. https://archive.org/details/DTIC_AD0475846

Barbrook, Richard, *Class Wargames: Ludic Subversion against Spectacular Capitalism*. Wivenhoe/New York/Port Watson: Minor Compositions, 2014.

Booth, Paul, *Board Games as Media*. New York: Bloomsbury, 2021.

Chatterjee, Partha, *Nationalist Thought and the Colonial World. A Derivative Discourse*. London: Zed Books, 1993.

von Clausewitz, Carl, *On War*, trans. Michael Howard and Peter Paret. Princeton: Princeton University Press. 1984.

Debord, Guy, *Le Jeu de la Guerre*. Paris: Gallimard, 2006 [1987].

Derbent, T., *Giap et Clausewitz*. Bruxelles: Éditions Aden, 2006.

Fanon, Frantz, *A Dying Colonialism*. New York City: Grove Press, 1967 [1959].

Fanon, Frantz, *Black Skin, White Masks*. New York City: Grove Press, 2008 [1952].

Ford, D., "eXplore, eXpand, eXploit, eXterminate': Affective Writing of Postcolonial History and Education in Civilization V.' *Game Studies*, 16(2), 2016.

Galula, David, *Counterinsurgency Warfare: Theory and Practice*. Westport: Praeger Security International, 1964.

Ginzburg, Carlo, *The Cheese and the Worms. The Cosmos of a Sixteenth-Century Miller*. Baltimore: Johns Hopkins University Press, 1980.

Glucksmann, André, *Le discours de la guerre*. Paris: L'Herne, 1967.

GMT, 'Coin series', https://www.gmtgames.com/c-36-coin-series.aspx#[PageNumber(0)|PageSize(50)|PageSort(Name)|DisplayType(Grid)], no date.

Gortzak, Yoav, 'Using Indigenous Forces in Counterinsurgency Operations: The French in Algeria, 1954–1962.' *Journal of Strategic Studies*, 32, 2009: 307–333.

Goscha, Christopher, *The Road to Dien Bien Phu: A History of the First War for Vietnam*. Princeton: Princeton University Press, 2022.

Guy, Emmanuel, *Le jeu de la guerre de Guy Debord. L'émancipation comme projet*. Paris: Éditions B42, 2020.

LaPensée, Elizabeth, 'Indigenous Board Game Design in *The Gift of Food*.' *Analog Game Studies*, 3(2), 2016.

Llopis, Noel, 'Luck in Games.' *Games from Within*, published on Aug. 6, 2013, https://gamesfromwithin.com/luck-in-games.

Loomba, Ania, *Colonialism/Postcolonialism*. London: Routledge, 1998.

Magnet, Shoshana, 'Playing at Colonization. Interpreting Imaginary Landscapes in the Videogame *Tropico*.' *Journal of Communication Inquiry*, 30(2), 2006: 142–162.

24 G. Alonge and R. Fassone

Matthews, Jason, 'Politics in Wargaming and Wargaming in Politics'. Georgetown University Wargaming Society, August 24, 2021. https://www.youtube.com/watch?v=ub2Nj6iKBbM

Mukherjee, Souvik, 'Playing Subaltern: Video Games and Postcolonialism.' *Games and Culture*, 13(5), 2018: 504–520.

Mukherjee, Souvik, *Videogames and Postcolonialism. Empire Plays Back*. London: Palgrave Macmillan, 2017.

Mukherjee, Souvik, and Hammar, Emil Lundedal, 'Introduction to the Special Issue on Postcolonial Perspectives in Game Studies.' *Open Library of Humanities*, 4(2), 2018: 1–14.

NLR Editors, 'Introduction to Glucksmann'. *New Left Review* I/49 (May-June 1968): 35–40.

Palmer, Nicholas, *The Best of Board Wargaming*. New York: Hippocrene Books, 1980.

Parashar, Swati, 'Terrorism and the Postcolonial 'State'.' In *Routledge Handbook of Postcolonial Politics*, edited by Olivia Rutazibwa and Robbie Shilliam, 110–125. London: Routledge, 2018.

Sonnleitner, Michael W., 'Of Logic and Liberation: Frantz Fanon on Terrorism.' *Journal of Black Studies*, 17(3), 1987: 287–304.

Train, Brian, *Colonial Twilight. The French-Algerian War, 1954–62*. Playbook, Hanford: GMT, 2017.

Train, Brian, and Volko Ruhnke, 'Chess, Go, and Vietnam: Gaming Modern Insurgency.' In *Zones of Control: Perspectives on Wargaming*, edited by Pat Harrigan and Matthew G. Kirschenbaum, 513–529. Cambridge: The MIT Press, 2016.

Wehrle, Cole, 'Affective Networks at Play: *Catan*, COIN, and *The Quiet Year*.' *Analog Game Studies*, 3(3), 2016.

Woods, Stewart, *Eurogames. The Design, Culture and Play of Modern European Board Games*. Jefferson: McFarland & Co., 2012.

References – games

Avalon Hill, *Guerrilla*. Analog game designed by Neal Schlaffer, 1994.

Avalon Hill, *Rise and Decline of the Third Reich*. Analog game designed by Don Greenwood and John Prados, 1993.

Avalon Hill, *We The People*. Analog game designed by Mark Herman, 1974.

Flying Buffalo, *Dien Bien Phu: Strategic Game of Indochina 1950-55*. Analog game designed by Guy R. Hail and Dana F. Lombardy, 1977.

GDW, *Citadel: The Battle of Dien Bien Phu*. Analog game designed by Frank Allan Chadwick, 1977.

GMT, *All Bridges Burning: Red Revolt and White Guard in Finland, 1917–1918*. Analog game designed by VPJ Arponen, 2020.

GMT, *Andean Abyss*. Analog game designed by Volko Ruhnke, 2012.

GMT, *Colonial Twilight: The French-Algerian War, 1954–62*. Analog game designed by Brian Train, 2017.

GMT, *Gandhi: The Decolonization of British India, 1917–1947*. Analog game designed by Bruce Mansfield, 2019.

GMT, *Twilight Struggle*. Analog game designed by Ananda Gupta and Jason Matthews, 2005.

Jeux Descartes, *Diên Biên Phu. La bataille decisive de la guerre d'Indochine*. Analog game designed by Jean-Luc Ancely, 1980.

Les Jeux Stratégiques et Historiques, *Le Jeu de la Guerre*. Analog game designed by Guy Debord, 1977.

PopTop Software, *Tropico*. Digital game designed by Phil Steinmeyer, 2001.

SPI, *South Africa: The Death of Colonialism*. Analog game designed by Irad B. Hardy, published by "Strategy and Tactics", 62 (May-June 1977).

Swedish Game Production, *Dien Bien Phu*. Analog game designed by Claes Henrikson, 1977.

3 Design Elements in Postcolonial Commercial Historical Board Wargames

Maurice Suckling

Introduction

Let us work with a broad definition of "postcolonial" – "all the culture affected by the imperial process from the moment of colonization to the present day" (Ashcroft, Griffiths, and Tiffin 1989, 2). Within this definition, the moment of colonization might not necessarily pertain only to the successful (from the perspective of the colonizer) completion of the act in any given polity, but also extends out to the process of attempted colonization. Indeed, the authors of that same broad definition also give us the definition of "post-colonialization" as "a process in which colonized societies participate over a long period, through different phases and modes of engagement with the colonizing power *during* and *after* the period of direct colonial rule (sic)" (Ashcroft, Griffiths, and Tiffin 2002, 195). The breadth of these definitions appears to permit an extension into the topics under consideration within this chapter. For further clarity, the forms of colonialism included in this focus pertain both to settler colonialism (Nayar 2015, 137), that is, those with a focus on assimilation and uniformity (Young 2015, 19–20), and exploitation colonies (Nayar 2015, 77), that is those with a focus on association and diversity (Young 2015, 19–20). Included too is the notion that: "[p]ostcolonial critique incorporates the legacy of the syncretic traditions of Marxisms that developed outside the west in the course of anti-colonial struggles, and subsequently in the development of the further forms of emancipation, of gender, ethnicity and class, necessary for liberation from bourgeois nationalism" (Young 2016, 10).

Dunnigan defines a wargame. "A wargame (manual or computer) usually combines a map, playing pieces representing historical personages or military units, and a set of rules telling you what you can or cannot do with them" (Dunnigan 1992, 13). Dunnigan expands this definition. "The object of any specific wargame (historical or otherwise) is to enable the player to re-create a specific event and, more important, to be able to explore what might have been if the player decides to do things differently" (Dunnigan 1992, 13). We might consider these "events" in Dunnigan's terms to be the "phases" Ashcroft, Griffiths, and Tiffin refer to within the context of a "long period", and

DOI: 10.4324/9781003356318-3

the "things players can and cannot do" with the military units would equate to the "modes of engagement". The term "wargame", whether historical in focus or not, is contentious within hobby circles and the definition can extend into political conflict, perhaps even to the exclusion of direct military action (Buchanan 2021, 46–47; Ruhnke 2021, 47). Dunnigan's "manual" term here intends what might otherwise be termed a "tabletop game" or a "board game" – a game played on a tabletop with a board, tokens and possibly cards, including their hybrid and fully digital versions. Postcolonial historical board wargames, then, are here deemed to be those that represent a specific conflict in a postcolonial situation (i.e. a former colony after the colonizing power has retreated or is in the process of retreating), or represent a specific conflict in a colonial situation (i.e. the land is still a colony) or in the process of being colonized, or resisting colonization, or those that attempt to adopt an anti-colonialist position, instead of reiterating colonial narratives deeply entrenched in the gaming tradition (No Pun Included 2021).

Whether bringing focus to bear on Roman Britain, or nineteenth-century British colonies of a "Greek" (settler) or "Roman" (exploitation) quality (Young 2015, 20) the relationship to agency and complexity (both political and military) seems to hold true as being postcolonial. Of particular relevance here is Young: "If colonial history, particularly in the nineteenth century, was the history of imperial appropriation of the world, the history of the twentieth century has witnessed the people of the world taking power and control back for themselves. Postcolonial theory is itself a product of that dialectical process" (Young 2016, 4). A key part of that "taking control back" is connected to the central notion of "writing back" (Sorensen 2010, 97) to reassert narratives that have been distorted or omitted by a colonial lens (Booth 2021, 179).

This chapter concerns itself with commercial historical board wargames such as those in GMT's *COIN* series (2012 onwards) – a focus in the preceding chapter, and *Pax Pamir* (Wehrlegig Games 2015, 2019), among several others. The central contention of this chapter is that within a game's setting as colonial or postcolonial, there are three key design elements that help us determine a game as "postcolonial":

- a strategic-level agency is given to a colonized/would-be colonized people,
- a representation of complex strategic-level asymmetries of multiple (e.g. political, cultural, economic, and technological) aspects of the historical situation, and
- a representation of conflict asymmetries between the colonized and colonizers modeled also on the operational and tactical levels.

This is the lens through which this chapter will explore specific design elements utilized in these games. Design elements explored here demonstrate ways in which designers have found to represent asymmetric capabilities, restrictions, and objectives, and ways to represent the asymmetry of information versus firepower, and the development of unintended consequences.

Strategic-Level Agency

As previously postulated by others (Mukherjee and Hammar 2018, 2; Ashcroft, Griffiths, and Tiffin 2013, 9–10) agency is a critical element within postcolonial enquiry. If an indigenous or colonized or would-be colonized or would-be exterminated people are given agency through being controlled by a player then a postcolonial perspective is possibly being adopted. If there is no such agency then it is almost certainly not. Janet Murray gives us "agency" as "…the satisfying power to take meaningful action and see the results of our decisions and choices" (Murray 1998, 216). With player agency comes an anointment of being deemed to matter, being deemed to be of such consequence that this people or polity had the capacity to make choices, however, constrained, and to therefore shape their own history. It is hard to see how a postcolonial perspective might be presented without this form of agency. Yet even if this agency is granted the game's setting may still be essentially colonial in aspect, according to the game's overall context. A game about a famous colonial battle may well fit more within a colonial narrative than a postcolonial one. This may still be the case, even if the battle was a victory for indigenous forces, because the battle may essentially fit within a broader colonial narrative of eventual conquest, and/or the forbearance of colonial troops. *Zulus on the Ramparts: The Battle of Rorke's Drift* (Victory Point Games 2009) is a solo game, played from the perspective of the British, against a game-system Zulu enemy. We can see this neatly fits within a colonial perspective. But two-player games like *Victoria Cross: The Battle of Rorke's Drift* (Worthington Games 2004), and *Victoria Cross II: Battle of Isandlwana & Rorke's Drift* (Worthington Games 2011) offer no significant perspective shift, because, although there is agency, the context within which the agency occurs is also critical. Agency in a tactical-level game may do no more than reinforce pre-existing colonial narratives wherein the indigenous people play a part in a narrative they do not control that is ultimately about their suppression or eradication. In a Rorke's Drift game, at a tactical level, the Zulus may have agency, but this is likely an invitation to play out a role in a colonialist script in a colonialist theater to an audience that is essentially colonialist in terms of its expectations. So, it is suggested here, for a wargame to be considered postcolonial, it must not only offer agency to the indigenous people or polity, but it must also do so within what is likely to be a strategic-level context that therefore gives that people or polity a meaningful way in which to exert that agency; a way that is not necessarily bound by an overarching colonial narrative of ultimate and inevitable suppression. Such a postcolonial treatment, then, would be to run contrary to Douglas' assertion about the digital game series *Civilization* (Microprose 1991 onwards) and how its "ultimate effect is to reinforce the pattern of interaction between the colonizing power and the aboriginal" (Douglas 2002).

Pax Pamir (first edition 2015, second edition 2019) is set in the "Great Game" of late nineteenth-century British and Russian imperial rivalry over Afghanistan. This is assuredly colonial in the setting. Yet here, players control neither empire. Instead, they control different Afghan leaders attempting to navigate toward survival through the fluctuating balance of power in the region. Players win by aligning their loyalty with the faction – British, Russian, or combined Afghan – that achieves supremacy. Such a treatment of a colonial setting is demonstrably postcolonial. It encourages agency which speaks to a complexity beyond a simplistic colonial narrative of imperial Britain good/strong; imperial Russia bad/weak, or vice versa.

Political Complexity

Indeed, a second key design element that defines postcolonialism here is some representation of political complexity, however lightly modeled. Colonial board wargames tend to be reductive about political modeling, framing the conflict as superior technology versus inferior technology (often few in number against many), "saving the colonies from their own 'backwardness'" (Borit, Borit, and Olsen 2018, 17). A colonial framing has a developed civilization confronting a primitive one – the "West over the Rest" as Hall terms it (Hall 2007, 221). A postcolonial framing allows for non-imperial perspectives, and grants, at the very least, the potential of an identity, validity, and complexity to this non-imperial political context on its own terms, it releases the player from being "forced to enact the narrative in a colonialist manner, concerned only with expansion and depleting resources" (Dillon 2008, 132). Thus *Pax Pamir* gives us not only a strategic-level agency that is postcolonial, it also presents a modeling of political complexity that is postcolonial too. (See Carr 2021, 40–41 for reference to "modeling" as a design concept.)

With this political modeling comes a deeper appreciation of strategic complexities. Representing political and strategic-level complexities leads to representing asymmetries, which can be hugely problematic for game designers, even putting aside the commercial viability of games with this design intention. Might a game where the military power of one faction – perhaps a controlling or colonizing faction – over a would-be colonized faction be so overwhelming that it delivers a game with poor balance and be poor entertainment? Assuredly so, but then a certain kind of game designer might also add it would also be poor history. For, most conflicts in history have been imbalanced, and yet few have been straightforward. Consider Afghanistan in the Nineteenth, Twentieth, and Twenty-First centuries, The Vietnam War, Napoleon's armies in Spain, or Russia … history is littered with famous examples of military superiority in some regards being combined with inferiority in some other regards. There are a great many more examples of less well-known conflicts with the same kind of marked asymmetries – the Mixton War (1540), the Zanj Rebellion (869), and the Iraq Revolt (1920) to name just three among an immensely long list of others. Indeed these "irregular" wars are really the default ways in which wars happen; they are really the "regular" way that wars are fought (Harrigan and Kirschenbaum 2016, 513). More advanced weaponry, and more resources do not guarantee victory. Speed of movement, security of and distance to supply depots, access to information, extent of local support, alliances, political will of participants and the willingness to suffer casualties, are all factors with a bearing on how a conflict might turn out. Some of these factors speak to political/strategic complexity, some relate more to operational/tactical military dynamics. Furthermore, as Kilcullen tells us: "Counterinsurgency is fundamentally a competition between many groups, each seeking to mobilize the population in support of their agenda - counterinsurgency is always more than two-sided" (Kilcullen 2006, 2). So how can a game designer, especially a commercial game designer who is balancing considerations like table space, component limitations, playability, and constrained play time, hope to confront these issues? Besides the approach taken in *Pax Pamir*, what other tools are available to designers?

The work of prolific designer Brian Train (born 1964) has focused on political and political-military conflict, rather than merely military conflict (BGG n.d.-c; Train 2022). His work has often taken subject matter of civil disturbance, and unconventional warfare, most often in reasonably recent and contemporary history. Among his 61 (at the time of writing) published titles listed on Boardgamegeek.com (BGG), we find *Tupamaro* (BTR Games 1995), is a 2-player strategic-level game about the conflict between the Tupamaro guerrillas and the Uruguayan State 1968-1972; *Shining Path: The Struggle for Peru* (BTR Games 1999), a 2-player strategic-level game about the conflict between the "Shining Path" Maoist guerrillas and the Peruvian State 1980 – ongoing; *Algeria: The War of Independence 1954–1962* (Microgame Design Group 2000), a 2-player strategic-level game about the conflict between the FLN nationalist guerrillas and the French government; *Kandahar* (BTR Games 2013), is a 2-player strategic-level game about the conflict between the Taliban and Afghan National Security forces in southern Afghanistan; *EOKA: The Cyprus Emergency 1935-1939* (BTR Games 2010), set during the conflict between the terrorist group EOKA (Ethnikí Orgánosis Kipriakoú Agónos, the National Organisation of Cypriot Struggle) and the security forces of the United Kingdom and the Government of Cyprus; and *Andartes: The Greek Civil War 1947-49* (BTR Games 2014), is a 2-player strategic-level game about the conflict between Communist-inspired guerrillas and the Greek State (BGG, n.d.-b).[1]

Tupamaro (BGG, n.d.-l), *Shining Path* (BGG, n.d.-k), *Algeria* (BGG, n.d.-a), *Kandahar* (BGG, n.d.-h), *EOKA* (BGG, n.d.-d), and *Andartes* (BGG, n.d.-b) all have different action menus, meaning a tailored list of possible actions for each faction involved. (A use of a mechanic Engelstein and Shalev term "Action Points" combined with one they term "Variable Player Powers" Engelstein and Shalev 2022, 77–80, and 106–107.) This design tool fusion allows for a means of modeling political complexity, asymmetry, and variety, but, equally, relates to operational and tactical asymmetries too. In the case of *Tupamaro,* the action menu is a list of available "missions" and which cover a range of political, strategic, operational, and tactical military options, police actions, and actions related to organized crime – a blend of kinetic and non-kinetic activities. Even without further explanation of these missions, presenting the list available for download on BGG should give some sense of the variety see Figure 3.1: *Tupamaro* Missions List.

This matrix demonstrates how some of these actions are bound by circumstance, so not all actions are always available ("Action Selection Restrictions", Engelstein and Shalev 2022, 104), and players must strategize in order to make actions available when they need them. The concept of these capabilities became more detailed and asymmetric as Train developed games subsequent to *Tupamaro* in the same "4-box family" – so named because each map has four boxes on it: UG (Underground insurgents), Ops (space for operations to be executed by both sides), Ops Comp (where pieces are placed after completing an operation), and PTL (a Patrol, where static forces wander and wait).

In addition, these games all use "political will", "support points", or some other similarly phrased concept as a central currency. The main currency in *Tupamaro* is the Political Support Level (PSL) measured from 0 to 99. Train elaborates thus:

It represents the level of support, commitment or legitimacy the mass of the civilian population is prepared to give one side or the other. During the game, each player maintains a PSL independently of the other. By showing this in a non-zero-sum fashion, we can model simply a highly polarized and committed society (where both sides would have a high PSL) or one overrun by fatigue, confusion or apathy (where both sides would have a low PSL), or something in between. And if your PSL hits zero, this implies some kind of final organizational collapse… you lose.[2]

This kind of *global game loss index* has a long lineage in board wargames. It goes back at least as far as *Viet Nam* (Gamescience 1965), where driving the index up, by capturing cities, brings a player closer to victory, and also unlocks further operational upgrades – such as additional replacements, additional movement capacity of air units, imposing movement restrictions for the enemy – which, in turn, assist the movement of the index further toward victory (BGG 2014). This kind of design approach in Train's work – to pull focus onto a key currency or index which determines loss ("Victory Points from Game State" Engelstein and Shalev 2022, 214) and calling it "Political

Tupa Mission	AP	Notes	Result	DRM
Build	3	Build 2 dummies per turn	Put one Fireteam in the Safe Zone. May be used this turn.	
Infiltrate	1~?	-1 AP for Neutral SSA; -2 or +3 AP for pro-Govt SSA	Remove Fireteam from Safe Zone and place Infiltrator in UG box	
Propaganda	1		≡ ≡ PSL to increase Tupa or decrease Govt (Tupa chooses); ≡ = Shift SSA alignment one level pro-Tupa	
Riot / Strike	4	Needs Infiltrator in SSA In Shops, Factories, Transport	≡ ≡ x .d6 PSL to increase Tupa or decrease Govt (Tupa chooses). If action was a Strike, may use points to reduce Economy + Fireteam captured or eliminated (Govt player chooses) -d6 Govt PSL if it does not React to one or more Riots Strikes	
Robbery	1	Only in SSA marked "R"	≡ = AP gained; + = Fireteam captured or eliminated (Govt player chooses)	-1 for Infiltrator; -1 per unit on Guard
Kidnap / Prison Break / Eliminate Informer	2~?	Only in SSA marked "K"; Only in Prison box	≡ = Kidnap/Prison Break: Informer Elimination is successful; roll d6 per unit: on ≤3 Prison Breaking unit gets to Safe Zone -d6 Govt PSL for Kidnap or successful Prison Break + = Fireteam captured or eliminated (Govt player chooses)	+1 for Infiltrator; +1 for Infiltrator; +1 per extra AP spent; -1 per unit on Guard
Intimidation	4	No React mission is allowed	≡ = points of morale of our organization; + or * = One Fireteam captured or eliminated (Govt player chooses)	-1 per extra Fireteam

Govt Mission	AP	Notes	Result	DRM
Build	2 per unit, 3 per unit if Expended Remove one Recruit	Appear immediately	Build Recruit class unit	
Train	1, -1 if Neutral, -2 or -3 if pro-Tupa Thereafter 1 per turn	Only 1 turn until first Crisis	Train Line and Elite, 2 turns delay	
Place Informer	1 per unit in Deployment Phase	Must maintain each turn	Place Informer in the SSA	
Guard		Place in Deployment Phase	Free React in SSA, then Expended	May Guard Prison
Cordon & Search	1 per unit, 2 per unit if Expended -1 to Govt PSL for a Recruit unit	Roll d6 per unit: ≤3 x Elite Units +; 2 x Line Units +; 1 x Recruit Units +	Flip unit face up; Destroy dummies and Infiltrators; May react against discovered units; Free discovered Kidnapped Figures	+2 vs UG unit; -1 for Informer; -1 for Elite unit; -1 Internal War declared
Intelligence	3	Roll d6 per unit: ≤3 is a result	Flip unit face up; Destroy dummies and Infiltrators; May react against discovered units	+1 vs UG unit; -1 for Informer; -1 Internal War declared
React	2 per unit, 3 per unit if Expended -1 to Govt PSL for a Recruit unit	Roll d6 per unit: ≥4: unit is captured	Units are captured or eliminated (Govt player chooses); Govt unit may stay in Guard circle	-1 for Informer; -1 for Elite unit

MISSION SUCCESS TABLE

DieRoll	-1	0	1	2	3	4	5	6	7	8
Result	0-	0-	1+	1	1	2	2	3+	4+	5+

Figure 3.1 Tupamaro Missions List (BGG 2003)

Note: SSAs are Social Sector Areas – abstracted out conceptual areas of the city of Montevideo, representing economic and social activity.

Support" or similar ensures military successes of all kinds are subservient to more overriding political agendas. Political will is contextualized as the fuel that powers agency, as well as being the defining element of defeat. You may not be able to win with high levels of political support, but you can surely lose if the levels plummet. With such an approach it is hard for players to fail to grasp the key concerns of the game.

Even in *Kandahar*, where Support Points (SPs) are not the key determinants of victory (Victory Points are), SPs are still the currency through which a faction fuels its activity, and the reduction of SPs to 0 still represents a "point of organizational crisis" and the game is lost.[3] *Kandahar* is also worthy of note in its representation of complexity by utilizing hidden objective cards ("End Game Bonuses" that are private goals, Engelstein and Shalev 2022, 225). These are kept secret from opposing players – although actions taken might mean the objective becomes increasingly obvious – and are worth VP if the criteria are met, but they can also change during the game – due to random events, or due to players attempting to swap out their card.

Train's work was a key inspiration for Volko Ruhnke's development of *Labyrinth: The War on Terror, 2001–?* (GMT Games 2010) and his subsequent and somewhat linked COIN (COunter INsurgency) series for GMT games (Beyond Solitaire Podcast 58, 2021; GMT 2015, 29).[4] Ruhnke has some considerable standing in this space, not only from the critical and commercial success of this series, but also from his career as a CIA national security analyst. As the preceding chapter also outlines, most of the games in the COIN series (2012 – ongoing at the time of writing) have political complexity represented through, in part, the multiplicity of factions. Most of these games are not 2-player but 4-player games, where each faction seeks victory not in any permanent alliance, but within a game system that permits them some means of shifting their support to other factions to ensure they alone ultimately come out ahead.[5] The concept of asymmetric capabilities and resources in the action menus in Train's earlier work is also a central design element in *Labyrinth* and the COIN series. A further development in the COIN series is the way these asymmetries of methods and means feed into asymmetric objectives (not hidden in these games).

A Distant Plain: Insurgency in Afghanistan (GMT Games 2013; BGG, 2013), designed by Train and Ruhnke, represents the political-military situation in Afghanistan 2002–2013. The game's four factions are the Coalition, the Government, the Taliban, and the Warlords. Their respective and clearly different objectives are listed below:

Coalition: Total Support + Available Coalition pieces – 30.

Government: COIN-Controlled Population + Patronage – 35.

Taliban: Total Opposition + Taliban Bases – 20.

Warlords: Lower of Uncontrolled Afghan Population – 15 or Warlord Resources – 40.

(GMT Games 2015, 11)

As may be discerned, these asymmetric objectives are complicated by their duality. Each faction has one *independent* objective, and one *dependent* objective, ensuring, here, an antagonistic relationship with one other faction. In the case of the Coalition objectives, the availability of Coalition pieces is independent – it is unrelated to the activities of other factions. The concept here is that one of the things the Coalition most wants is to withdraw its troops, so it is critically penalized for bringing/leaving too many troops in the region, i.e. it is unable to win if it does so. However, the other thing the Coalition most wants – its other objective – is to ensure there is sufficient support for the Government. Yet, in order to achieve this objective, the Coalition will come into conflict with another faction – in this case, The Taliban - which has its own objective of ensuring that opposition to the Government is sufficiently high. For the Coalition and the Taliban, this is an intersection of dependent objectives. For the Coalition the dilemma is that having troops in Afghanistan is how it drives up support for the Government and so seeks to attain its dependent objective, but having troops out of Afghanistan is how it fulfills its other – independent – objective. Similarly, the Government and the Warlords have their own independent objectives, but their own intersecting dependent objectives over the control of the population. Such a configuration can ensure "perverse incentives" develop for factions to cooperate in unexpected ways (S3 US West 2015, 26).[6]

The COIN system utilizes the mission menu system seen in Train's earlier work, and breaks available actions into two kinds – perhaps called Operations, for certain standard type activities like movement and combat, and Special Activities, for rarer activities, such as airlifts, or air strikes. (The names of these types of activities vary within the series – they are called "Commands" and "Feats" in *Pendragon: The Fall of Roman Britain*, 2017, for example.) We shall look closer at these action menus as we consider operational and tactical asymmetries in the following section. But there is a strategic-level significance to these action menus in COIN, because the choices made by a player have an impact not only on other players, but also on the player making the choice.

At the beginning of the game all player factions are "1st Eligible Factions". After the first round of play, each player faction is either the "1st Eligible Faction", "2nd Eligible Faction", or "Ineligible". 1st Eligible factions may choose to select a Command action, or Command + Special Ability, or to implement the current Event card for one of its usually two mirrored effects, or it may Pass. If the 1st Eligible Faction chooses a Command action, the 2nd Eligible Faction may only make a Limited Command action or Pass. If the 1st Eligible Faction chooses a Command + Special Ability, the 2nd Eligible Faction may choose the Event, or a Limited Command action, or Pass. If the 1st Eligible Faction chooses the Event, the 2nd Eligible Faction may choose a Command + Special Ability, or Pass. If the 1st Eligible

Faction chooses to Pass, the 2nd Eligible Faction may choose Limited Command, Event or Limited Command, or Command + Special Ability, or Pass. If the 1st Eligible Faction chooses to Pass it retains its 1st Eligible status, and receives some Resources, otherwise its status will switch to ineligible. (A blend of "Lose A Turn" and "Action Drafting" mechanics, Engelstein and Shalev 2020, 66–67, 74–75.)

The COIN Event deck needs further explanation. The COIN system is card-assisted, rather than card-driven. Player actions are largely determined by the action menus, not by the cards they hold in their hand. But the sequence of play includes the reveal of the top card of the Event deck. The top of this card indicates the order in which factions take their turns in the present round - if, indeed, they are to get a turn in the present round. This order is randomized throughout the card deck, thus adding the mechanic Engelstein and Shalev would call "Random Turn Order" to the "Lose A Turn" and "Action Drafting" mechanics to this system (Engelstein and Shalev 2020, 55–56). Within this Event deck are a number of "Propaganda" cards (this number may vary, but in *A Distant Plain* there are 6 Propaganda cards and 72 Event cards, and there is 1 Propaganda card shuffled into each sub-deck of 12 cards, which are then stacked, so that every 12 cards there is a Propaganda card, but it's placement could be anywhere within that 12). Once drawn, these Propaganda cards cause players to immediately check if any faction has met its victory conditions, in which case the game has a winner and immediately ends. (An example of Victory Points from Game State triggered by Random Systems, Engelstein and Shalev 2022, 214–215.)

But what does this all represent – this Propaganda card-laden Event deck integrated with player action menu options with their own eligibility status, together with the resultant flux of turn order? It appears three key elements of unconventional warfare are being represented through these integrated systems: the nature of unintended consequences, the decentering of time, and the trade-off between firepower versus intelligence. Ruhnke elaborates on the first of these topics:

> I believe that the accumulation of long-term effect as well as unintended consequences are particularly salient features of insurgency and counterinsurgency. The COIN Series tries to bring such features out in a variety of ways. First, critical, cumulative effects are assessed at semi-random intervals via "Propaganda" cards that punctuate campaigns representing a year or two. Much player blow-by-blow during the campaigns aims to build toward the Propaganda round, to be able then to influence the population, garner resources, or perhaps even score a victory through an overwhelming position. Many individual player decisions also incorporate short- versus long-term objectives and gains, such as whether to crimp operational tempo with training effort or deployment of a unique capability. Finally, the nature of most

event cards—each a dual option that players will have to expend effort in order to guide in the direction favorable to them—in part represent unintended consequences.

(Grogheads 2012)

With the turn sequence not being guaranteed there are clear ramifications on the ability to affect strategy. Plans are begun, then aborted, due to an unexpected move by the enemy, but each faction's plans are frequently unsettled or contorted by each other in the strategic flux. Not only does this represent the staccato rhythm of irregular warfare, but it also reflects how formulated plans with clear intentions may be frustrated by the surprise plans of competing factions, or how all plans might be countermanded by the presentation of enticing opportunities. In this way, the game system demonstrates the way unintended consequences can unfold through complex causalities. In addition, this system also demonstrates how complications arise to undermine the certainty of a carefully regulated "colonial" framework of time (Ganguly 2004, 162). Instead, there is no simple plan-to-execution cycle of causality. This is a postcolonial framework of time. Causality is complicated by a multitude of plans begun and partially executed spawning new reactions and counter-reactions none of which might be fully executed before new developments unfold. Ruhnke elaborates further:

> Regarding the particular structure and content of the Andean Abyss [action] menus, I wanted to get at the importance of semi-random initiative in the moving and spooking between guerrillas and counter-insurgent forces, to help get at the information advantage versus firepower advantage, a core concept of insurgency. So the cards would provide the random initiative order each turn, but the players could decide somewhat where to go for an action and how much of a response to give the enemy. This is on the premise that it takes you longer and more focus to do bigger things, so your enemy meanwhile will get to do bigger things too. That's the origin of the COIN series' [a] sequence of play that interacts with the action menus and the Events at the same time.[7]

So, the focus of a "big" response such as from Command + Special Activity may put the enemy on the backfoot, with their own immediate response being limited, but it will come at the cost of the player missing a turn, and on the second turn being the 2nd Eligible faction. In addition, in order to be in a position to make a "big play" like a Command + Special Activity in the first place, that faction must already have got itself into the position of being the 1st Eligible faction, which means it has previously not made "big plays", or the enemy itself has made "big plays" of their own.

In this design of a system in which we demonstrate instability and degrees of unpredictability, we might see some attempt to encapsulate the postcolonial as an alternative to the "Imperial Mode" cited by Meghna Jayanth, at least with regards to "achieving mastery over the game's systems" (Jayanth 2022).

Operational and Tactical Asymmetries

Beyond political and strategic dynamics touched on above, the COIN system also represents operational and tactical asymmetries through the specifics of the action menu, which tend to be operational/tactical in focus in COIN, rather than the mixture seen in Train's solo work. In *A Distant Plain*, these action menu options are as follows:

Coalition: Operations – Sweep, Train, Assault, Patrol; Special Activities: Surge, Air Strike, Air Lift.

Government: Operations – Sweep, Train, Assault, Patrol; Special Activities: Govern, Transport, Eradicate.

Taliban: Operations – Rally, Attack, Terror, March; Special Activities: Extort, Ambush, Infiltrate.

Warlords: Operations – Rally, Attack, Terror, March; Special Activities: Cultivate, Traffic, Suborn.

(GMT Games 2015, 6–9)

Without delving deeper into detail here about what these specific actions permit, they might give a sufficient sense of the asymmetries in their names alone. It should further be stated, that in order to choose one of these actions not only must the circumstances in the sequence of play align (with regards to eligibility to perform certain actions at a given time), but that specific Special Activities can only be combined with specific Operations, and that, most of the time there is a specific Resource requirement (another index tracked on the board, and a measure of a faction's wherewithal to effect Operations) which must be paid in order for the action to be chosen. In addition, there are always spatial obligations to be fulfilled too – relevant units must be in relevant locations at the appropriate times in order for the action to be feasible ("Action Selection Restrictions" Engelstein and Shalev 2022, 104–105).

Beyond these playability parameters the various player actions are also operating within a matrix of counterbalancing "design levers". This is a system of push-me, pull-me options that permit an operational/tactical implementation of political and strategic-level incentives. This matrix can be visually demonstrated on the *Faction Interactions Chart* (see S3 US West 2015, 16). Even without fully grasping the details of how the game systems work, this chart clearly demonstrates the ways in which factions can help, or more often, hinder the success of other factions, and gives some sense of the system's capacity to represent operational complexity and the asymmetric nature of interactions.

There is one further design element in COIN (and also in the precursor *Labyrinth*) which speaks to operational/tactical complexity and asymmetry. Both *Labyrinth* and COIN utilize a novel concept of masked presence – a specific use of "Hidden Information" (Engelstein and Shalev 2022, 288-89). This is an approach whereby specific "irregular" units (Jihadist plotters or fighters in *Labyrinth,* Taliban or Warlord guerrillas in *A Distant Plain*) are seen on the board by players, but these units are invulnerable until unmasked through counter-insurgency actions, or through the violent actions of these units themselves. The wooden pieces representing the respective pieces are embossed at one end. When inverted, with the embossed end face down on the board the pieces are masked. When the pieces are placed embossed face up it indicates they are now unmasked, and so visible, and vulnerable. This approach allows designers to evoke the cat-and-mouse nature of irregular warfare, with stealth and concealment being a key weapon in the armory of insurgents, and vulnerability to counter-insurgent forces once their position is revealed being a key factor in favor of counterinsurgent forces.

Rebellion: Britannia, a game in development with GMT Games (forthcoming) at the time of writing, clearly inspired by COIN in more ways than one, utilizes the same basic approach of masked presence as the distinction is made between Tension and Warbands, flipping the same disc's face to represent either (political) Tension or a (military) Warband (BGG n.d.-j). In *Rebellion: Britannia,* the Rome faction attempts to win victory points largely by building settlements and forts, and by attaining – however fleeting – military control of regions of Britannia, and will win pitched battles with Warbands, but cannot use those legions to confront Tension. Instead, they must use other approaches to reduce Tension, some of which are directly counter to how they otherwise gain victory points - such as by building, and marching legions into regions to gain military control. Similarly, the Briton factions can hurt Roman legions if they use Warbands, but Tension is of no direct military value. Yet developing sufficient Tension is how the Briton factions generate Warbands (only political support leads to military manifestation), which can ensure military dominance. So, the Briton players are frequently looking to turn Tension into Warbands, to score points, and then to revert back to Tension before the Romans can find and destroy them in battle (Paizomen 2021).

The COIN system is immensely rich in terms of the design tools it offers designers. Yet there are other, less complex systems that can assist in postcolonial board wargame design. *Conflict of Wills: Judean Hammer: Guerrilla Warfare During the Maccabean Revolt* (Catastrophe Games 2021) delivers operational asymmetry through recruitment, movement, ambushes, and supply. With regards to recruitment, the Maccabeans, insurgents in this game, are able, with some penalties, to recruit their units in any location on the map, whereas the Seleucid Greeks are restricted to supply centers, Greek-controlled cities, or areas adjacent to Greek-controlled cities in Greek-controlled regions. The Maccabeans, being guerrilla fighters, can move each unit 3 areas, and may not enter Greek supply centers, whereas the Greeks can move each unit in only 2 areas. In addition, Maccabeans can conduct ambushes which can compel Greek units to halt their movement and fight. The way ambushes are resolved ensures a 50% chance an ambush will be successful. Greek units are especially penalized by the supply rule – they must be able to trace an unbroken supply line to a Greek supply center. Indeed, much of the game revolves around the Maccabeans attempting to cut off Greek supply – especially to centrally located regions, Jerusalem in particular, and the Greeks endeavoring to keep the supply lines open (Catastrophe Games 2021). In 12 pages of rules, including historical and design notes, and a double-page spread with an annotated graphic of the board, in a large font size with numerous other graphics, *Judean Hammer* (BGG, n.d.-g) is a far different proposition than the work of Train or Ruhnke, clearly intended to deliver a different kind of play experience. Nevertheless, these simple implementations deliver on design intentions to represent operational asymmetries.

Patrick Rael takes Bogost's concept of procedural rhetoric – a concept of meaning carried through processes – and describes ludic rhetoric as that which "describes the argument made by the actual play procedures the game asks you to undertake" (Bogost 2008, 117–140; Rael 2019, 11). Rael contrasts this with discursive rhetoric, which he describes as "the way a game makes its argument through words unrelated to how you actually play" (Rael 2019, 10). Rael outlines discursive rhetorical elements as the introduction to the rulebook, informal appendices, or flavor text on cards. This distinction appears useful. Perhaps an adjacent term, offered here, might be "experiential rhetoric", to represent not so much the procedures within the design but what a player might extract from them. Such a term might complement Booth's "ludo-textual" to fuse "pure textual analysis with an additive of interactive and participatory elements" (Booth 2021, 19), and what Lankoski and Björk refer to as "playing a game and forming an understanding [of] how the game system works" (Lankoski and Björk 2015, 23). So, if a COIN game elicits discomfort, perhaps even stress through the flux in the sequence of play, and/or through the difficulty in coordinating through the intersection of game systems to satisfy victory conditions then this is an extraction from the designed systems residing in the experience of the player. (See "Formal Analysis of Gameplay" in Lankoski and Björk 2015, 23–35). It seems prudent to distinguish between the argument the game appears to be making - bearing in mind there are difficulties here (if the game is played poorly what are we to make of the argument understood by the player?) – and the experience felt by a player from their encounter of the game systems. Essentially this same concept has been previously referred to, specifically in relation to historical games, as the "elixir of experiential historiography" and is offered here for consideration of its potential efficacy in this field (Suckling 2017, 110–119). This, in turn, appears to resonate with what Booth called "studying games as activities", and what Stenros and Waern referred to as the active creation of a game session through the game system (Booth 2021, 9–10).

Conclusion

The discussion carried here is not intended as exhaustive on the design elements in postcolonial games. This is intended as a brief introduction to some of the more interesting and successful ways designers have brought design elements to bear in postcolonial frameworks. Even in the work of Train and Ruhnke there is more to say. Nothing has hitherto been said here about the way *Tupamaro* and *Shining Path* both allow for the changing nature of their respective conflicts over time. They both have security forces that begin at Recruit level, but can be trained to two different levels of greater competency (Harrigan and Kirschenbaum 2016, 521). Very little has been said about the way Train has approached the design of conceptual space for many of his designs, to focus on abstracted concepts over spatial realities. In his large body of work, Train has also devised systems beyond the ones largely covered here. There are other designers too – although not many who have concentrated on recent irregular wars. Aside from Train and Ruhnke, the work of Joe Miranda (BGG, n.d.-f), and Javier Romero (BGG, n.d.-e) warrants closer attention. The aforementioned *Viet Nam*, by Phil Orbanes – although extremely hard to find, even in the deeper recesses of the hobby – also warrants a closer look at its design elements. As Train and Ruhnke themselves note:

> It was meant for team play, and players could win either by a diplomatic victory or a military victory. Rules included simultaneous and hidden movement, a government stability index, world opinion, terrorism, ambushes, air strikes, and psychological warfare - all in a four-page rulebook.
>
> (Harrigan and Kirschenbaum 2016, 514)

There is also new work to examine too. Although no publisher has yet been announced for *Liberation – Haiti: a cooperative game of rebellion and abolition* the game's BGG listing suggests one may be soon confirmed (BGG n.d.-i). *Haiti* is a postcolonial board wargame among several other postcolonial board games, not all concerned with military matters, which was developed through the Zenobia Award scheme which ran through 2021 designed to promote board game design within marginalized groups (Zenobia, n.d.). Perhaps it may be little surprise that Ruhnke was such a significant catalyst for this initiative when the approach within his designs has been so open to a plethora of narratives and perspectives.

Notes

1 *Tupamaro* incorrectly listed as 2001 on BGG (n.d.-l), but this is a later edition.
2 Private correspondence, 2022. This text also closely matches the description in the rules of *Tupamaro*, from the Word file also made available to the author through private correspondence, 2022.
3 *Kandahar* rules, from private correspondence, 2022.
4 Also acknowledged in private correspondence, 2022.
5 Even when playable solo, these games have non-player flowcharts to deliver a form of AI to ensure as much faction agency complexity within the system is rendered as possible.
6 Train's own phrase.
7 Personal correspondence, 2022.

References – books and articles

Ashcroft, Bill, Griffin, Gareth, and Tiffin, Helen. 1989. *The Empire Writes Back: Theory and Practice in Post-Colonial Literatures.* First edition. London. Routledge.

Ashcroft, Bill, Griffin, Gareth, and Tiffin, Helen. 2002. *The Empire Writes Back: Theory and Practice in Post-Colonial Literatures.* Second edition. London. Routledge.

Ashcroft, Bill, Griffin, Gareth, and Tiffin, Helen. 2013. *Postcolonial Studies: The Key Concepts.* Third edition. London. Routledge.

Beyond Solitaire Podcast 58. Volko Ruhnke and Brian Train on *A Distant Plain.* Accessed September 6, 2022. https://www.youtube.com/watch?v=znyV4F7EgBg&t=1818s

BGG. April 10, 2013. "A Distant Plain: Image". BoardGameGeek.com. Accessed September 6, 2022. https://boardgamegeek.com/image/1632054/distant-plain

BGG. December 18, 2003. "Tupamaro Mission doc." BoardGameGeek.com. Accessed September 6, 2022. https://boardgamegeek.com/filepage/4190/tupamaro-missionsdoc

BGG. September 30, 2014. "Viet Nam. Image." BoardGameGeek.com. Accessed September 27, 2022. https://boardgamegeek.com/image/2255261/viet-nam

BGG. n.d.-a. "Algeria: The War of Independence 1954–1962." BoardGameGeek.com. Accessed September 6, 2022. https://boardgamegeek.com/boardgame/11293/algeria-war-independence-1954-1962

BGG. n.d.-b. "Andartes: The Greek Civil War 1947–49." BoardGameGeek.com. Accessed September 6, 2022. https://boardgamegeek.com/boardgame/158450/andartes-greek-civil-war-1947-49

BGG. n.d.-c. "Brian Train." BoardGameGeek.com. Accessed September 6, 2022. https://boardgamegeek.com/boardgamedesigner/1678/brian-train

BGG. n.d.-d. "EOKA." BoardGameGeek.com. Accessed September 6, 2022. https://boardgamegeek.com/boardgame/214564/eoka

BGG. n.d.-e. "Javier Romero." BoardGameGeek.com. Accessed September 6, 2022. https://boardgamegeek.com/boardgamedesigner/1477/javier-romero

BGG. n.d.-f. "Joseph Miranda." BoardGameGeek.com. Accessed September 6, 2022. https://boardgamegeek.com/boardgamedesigner/337/joseph-miranda

BGG. n.d.-g. "Judean Hammer." BoardGameGeek.com. Accessed September 6, 2022. https://boardgamegeek.com/boardgame/326998/judean-hammèr

BGG. n.d.-h. "Kandahar." BoardGameGeek.com. Accessed September 6, 2022. https://boardgamegeek.com/boardgame/163603/kandahar

BGG. n.d.-i. "Liberation: Haiti." BoardGameGeek.com. Accessed September 6, 2022. https://boardgamegeek.com/boardgame/349773/liberation-haiti

BGG. n.d.-j. "Rebellion: Britannia." BoardGameGeek.com. Accessed September 6, 2022. https://boardgamegeek.com/boardgame/363275/rebellion-britannia

BGG. n.d.-k. "Shining Path: The Struggle for Peru." BoardGameGeek.com. Accessed September 6, 2022. https://boardgamegeek.com/boardgame/7337/shining-path-struggle-peru

BGG. n.d.-l. "Tupamaro." BoardGameGeek.com. Accessed September 6, 2022. https://boardgamegeek.com/boardgame/7448/tupamaro

Bogost, I. 2008. "The Rhetoric of Video Games." In: Salen, K (Ed.), *The Ecology of Games: Connecting Youth, Games, and Learning*, 117–140. The John D. and Catherine T. MacArthur Foundation Series on Digital Media and Learning. Cambridge, MA: MIT Press.

Borit, Cornel, Borit, Melania, and Olsen, Petter. 2018. Representations of Colonialism in Three Popular, Modern Board Games: *Puerto Rico, Struggle of Empires*, and *Archipelago. Open Library of Humanities*, 4(1): 17. Accessed September 26, 2022 https://olh.openlibhums.org/article/id/4474/#!

Booth, Paul. 2021. *Board Games as Media*. London: Bloomsbury.

Buchanan, Harold. "That's Not a Wargame!" C3i, 2021.

Carr, Jason. "What is Game Development?" C3i, 2021.

Catastrophe Games. 2021. "Judean Hammer" rules.

Dillon, Beth A. 2008. Signifying the West: Colonialist Design in Age of Empires III: The Warchiefs. *Eludamos*, 2(1): 129–44. Accessed September 26, 2022 https://septentrio.uit.no/index.php/eludamos/article/view/vol2no1-10/5838

Douglas, Christopher. 2002. 'You Have Unleashed a Horde of Barbarians!': Fighting Indians, Playing Games, Forming Disciplines. *Postmodern Culture*, 13(1).

Dunnigan, James F. 1992. *The Complete Wargames Handbook: How to Play, Design, & Find Them*. New York, NY. Quill William Morrow.

Engelstein, Geoffrey and Shalev, Isaac. 2020. *Building Blocks of Tabletop Game Design: An Encyclopedia of Mechanisms*. First edition. Boca Raton, FL: CRC Press.

Engelstein, Geoffrey and Shalev, Isaac. 2022. *Building Blocks of Tabletop Game Design: An Encyclopedia of Mechanisms*. Second edition. Boca Raton, FL: CRC Press.

Ganguly, Keya. 2004. "Temporality and Postcolonial Critique." In: Lazarus, Neil (Ed.), *The Cambridge Companion to Postcolonial Literary Studies*. Cambridge: Cambridge University Press.

GMT Games. 2015. Accessed September 27, 2022. https://www.gmtgames.com/adistantplain/ADP-RULES-2015.pdf

Grogheads. August 2012. Accessed September 6, 2022. http://grogheads.com/int-adp2.html

Hall, Stuart 2007. "The West and the Rest: Discourse and Power." In: Das Gupta, T (Ed.), *Race and Racialization: Essential Readings*, 184–227. Toronto: Canadian Scholars Press.

Harrigan, P. and Kirschenbaum, M. (Eds.) 2016. *Zones of Control: Perspectives on Wargaming*. Cambridge, MA: MIT.

Jayanth, Meghna. 2022. "Game Design in the Imperial Mode #CGSA 2022." Medium.com. https://medium.com/@betterthemask/game-design-in-the-imperial-mode-cgsa-2022-e5a9a6a57859

Kilcullen, D. 2006. "Twenty-Eight Articles: Fundamentals of Company Level Counter-insurgency." https://smallwarsjournal.com/documents/28articles.pdf
Lankoski, Petri and Björk, Staffan. 2015. "Formal Analysis of Gameplay." In: Lankoski, P and Björk, S (Eds.), *Game Research Methods.* Philadelphia, PA. ETC Press.
Mukherjee, Souvik and Hammar, Emil L. 2018. Introduction to the Special Issue on Postcolonial Perspectives in Game Studies. *Open Library of Humanities*, 4(2):33, pp. 1–14. https://doi.org/10.16995/olh.309
Murray, J. H. 1998. *Hamlet on the Holodeck.* Cambridge, MA: MIT Press.
Nayar, Pramod K. 2015. *The Postcolonial Studies Dictionary.* Chichester: Wiley.
No Pun Included. "Colonialism – The Board Game Struggle." February 19, 2021. Accessed September 27, 2022. https://youtu.be/VQuFSxs9VXA
Paizomen. October 8, 2021. Accessed September 27, 2022. https://paizomen.com/2021/10/08/rebellion-britannia-1-the-game-by-maurice-suckling/
Rael, Patrick. 2019. "Pax Exasperation." Accessed September 6, 2022. https://tildesites.bowdoin.edu/~prael/Rael-Pax-Exasperation.pdf
Ruhnke, Volko. "What is a Wargame?" C3i, 2021.
S3 US West. Accessed September 6, 2022. https://s3-us-west-2.amazonaws.com/gmtwebsiteassets/adistantplain/ADP-PLAYBOOK-2015.pdf
Sorensen, Eli P. 2010. *Postcolonial studies and the literary: theory, interpretation and the novel.* Basingstoke, New York: Palgrave Macmillan.
Suckling, Maurice W. 2017. "Board With Meaning." *CEA Critic* 79(1).
Train, Brian. Homepage updated September 22, 2022. Accessed September 27, 2022. https://brtrain.wordpress.com/personal-ludography/
Young, Robert J. C. 2015. *Empire, Colony, Postcolony.* Chichester: Wiley.
Young, Robert J. C. 2016. *Postcolonialism: An Historical Introduction.* Chichester: Wiley.
Zenobia. n.d. Accessed September 6, 2022. https://zenobiaaward.org/

References - games

BTR Games, One Small Step, Schultze Games, *Tupamaro.* Analog game designed by Brian Train, 1995.
BTR Games, Microgame Design Group, One Small Step, *Shining Path: The Struggle for Peru.* Analog game designed by Brian Train, 1999.
BTR Games, *EOKA: The Cyprus Emergency 1935-1939,* Analog game designed by Brian Train, 2010.
BTR Games, One Small Step, *Kandahar.* Analog game designed by Brian Train, 2013.
BTR Games, *Andartes: The Greek Civil War 1947–49.* Analog game designed by Brian Train, 2014.
Catastrophe Games, *Conflict of Wills: Judean Hammer: Guerrilla Warfare During the Maccabean Revolt,* analog game designed by Robin David, 2021.
Gamescience, *Viet Nam. Analog game designed by Phil Orbanes,* 1965.
GMT Games, *Labyrinth: The War on Terror, 2001-?* Analog game designed by Volko Ruhnke, 2010.
GMT Games, *A Distant Plain: Insurgency in Afghanistan.* Analog game designed by Brian Train and Volko Ruhnke, 2013.

44   *M. Suckling*

GMT Games, *Pendragon: The Fall of Roman Britain*. Analog game designed by Morgane Gouyon-Rety, 2017.

GMT Games, *Rebellion: Britannia*. Analog game designed by Daniel Burt and Maurice Suckling, forthcoming.

Microgame Design Group, Platinum Dragon Productions, *Algeria: The War of Independence 1954-1962*. Analog game designed by Brian Train, 2000.

Microprose, *Civilization*. Computer game designed by Sid Meier and Bruce Shelley, 1991.

No publisher currently listed, *Liberation - Haiti: a cooperative game of rebellion and abolition*. Analog game designed by Damon Stone, forthcoming.

Victory Point Games, *Zulus on the Ramparts: The Battle of Rorke's Drift*. Analog game designed by Joseph Miranda, 2009.

Wehrlegig Games, *Pax Pamir*. Analog game designed by Cole Wehrle, first edition 2015, second edition 2019.

Worthington Games, *Victoria Cross: The Battle of Rorke's Drift*. Analog game designed by Grant Wylie and Mike Wylie, 2004.

Worthington Games, *Victoria Cross II: Battle of Isandlwana & Rorke's Drift*. Analog game designed by Grant Wylie and Mike Wylie, 2011.

4 Colonialist and Anti-Colonialist Play in *Spirit Island*

A Ludo-Textual Analysis

Andrew Kemp-Wilcox

Introduction

How should a board game, itself emerging from a historical tradition of systems reifying and privileging capitalist and colonialist ideology, declare open war on colonialist themes? In acknowledging the domination of colonialist historical and ahistorical play, can a well-meaning game designer successfully design a path through the complex challenges of anti-colonialist design? Understanding the difficulties designers face when approaching these tasks has been the work of postcolonial game studies for years, as researchers work to expose the colonialist assumptions and the weight of hegemonic design traditions that inform and constrain many historical games (Chapman, Foka, and Westin 2017, 358–371; Borit, Borit, and Olsen 2018, 1–40). However, as Soraya Murray (2018, 4) has pointed out, the work of postcolonial game studies must necessarily extend beyond analyzing and complicating colonialist tropes in gaming. Designers and game industry professionals who desire to move the form in new postcolonial (here meaning after or beyond the colonial) and anti-colonial directions require fresh directions and innovative approaches, and media analyses of board games that focus on player experience and the relationship between design and play can bolster the tools available to game designers seeking a new start for the medium in a postcolonial direction.

The 2017 board game *Spirit Island* is a significant example of a game that acknowledges and attempts to reject its colonialist lineage by presenting a counterfactual and ahistorical fantasy of anti-colonialist defense. *Spirit Island* offers players an opportunity to right a fictionalized historical wrong by taking control of one of the various mythical spirits that populate a fantastical island under siege by colonialist invaders. The game places players in the perspective of the colonized and offers them an appealing power fantasy. As godlike spirits, the players tap into the energy of the island and repel the colonial invaders using magic, natural disaster, and fear. Through play, the island is either saved from destructive settler colonialism or overrun with invaders and the corrupting pollution of their presence, referred to

DOI: 10.4324/9781003356318-4

in the game as blight. Since its release, *Spirit Island* has enjoyed a significant presence in the board gaming community. The game has produced a
handful of expansions—*Branch and Claw* (2017), *Jagged Earth* (2020), and
Feather and Flame (2022)—that provide additional gameplay mechanics,
spirits, and invaders, as well as a handful of gaming convention exclusives
and promotional spirits sought-after as board gaming collectibles. But even
without those expansions, the base game remains extremely popular. As of
this writing, *Spirit Island* is ranked 11th all-time in player rating on the hobbyist site boardgamegeek.com with an average rating of 8.4 out of 10. The
game is famous enough to become one of the signature titles of postcolonial
and anti-colonial design trends and is routinely cited in countless forums
and discussions on the topic, such as on the r/boardgames forum (Reddit
2020). Therefore, *Spirit Island* remains an essential and important text for
examining design strategies for anti-colonialist play, but also player experience and expectation of the same. If *Spirit Island* is a game that approaches
colonialism critically, then analysis of the game as a text can help to reveal
what assumptions about colonialism and anti-colonialism are endemic to
games, both in communities of play and design. This study will concern
itself only with the core boxed edition of *Spirit Island* and not its many
expansions, since that is the text most likely to be encountered and experienced by most players.

   As a method, this chapter will draw heavily from Paul Booth's *Board
Games as Media*, which proposes to move board game analysis into the
realm of media studies, including what Booth describes as ludo-textual
analysis (Booth 2021, 17–37), a technique that extends beyond what
Booth perceives as surface-level textual examination of the components
of board games and into a more open and dynamic understanding of how
games function as useful objects. Ludo-textual analysis is meant to examine play strategies and lived experience as facilitated and encouraged
by the rules and components of the game, with the goal of finding an analytical tool for play itself, sometimes elusively obscured in board game studies by its ephemeral emergence. Booth's method shares similarities with Ian
Bogost's concept of "procedural rhetoric" in digital games (Bogost 2010, 10),
which argues that systems and mechanics carry with them ideologies and
promote particular play experiences, ultimately making arguments in favor of those ideologies. Booth argues that board games create conditions
and systems that promote advantageous adoption of the game's embedded
ideologies, what Darshana Jayemanne would call "felicitous" play (Jayemanne
2018, 1–30).

   Critically, Booth hopes that ludo-textual analysis will provide board
game studies—itself already a less-trafficked corridor in game studies overall—an avenue to consider its objects as media texts. In that way, Booth
aligns his work with several recent additions to media studies literature
that theorize a more active and co-creative role for the media user in the

constitution of media experiences. For example, Daniel Reynolds proposes that digital games reveal the blurred and unstable borders between the mental and physical activity of a player and the actual lived and experienced media text (Reynolds 2019). My proposal for this analysis is that by allowing ludo-textual analysis to similarly complicate, obscure, or even eradicate the perceived borders between players and aspirational anti-colonialist media texts like *Spirit Island*, we gain an insightful tool for incorporating subjective play into broader examinations of textual meaning. Such an approach allows us to explore how the player's personal relationship with colonial tropes blend inseparably with a designer's choices and the publisher's industrial concerns to construct a coherent point of view on anti-colonialism and the history and heritage of colonial ideology within the media form itself. If such a broadly comprehensive picture could be sketched, critics and designers might develop better strategies for moving the board game medium beyond that colonialist heritage for good.

"You Are Powerful ..."

Surely, as a chapter in a volume dedicated to postcolonial board game studies, any attempt to establish the colonial history of board games would be redundant. Suffice to say that the development of the contemporary board game progressed alongside the innovation of mechanics that abstract and gamify colonial and capitalist practices, from the war and strategy simulations of the nineteenth-century *kriegsspiel* (Peterson 2012, 212–251) to the resource and colonization play of *The Settlers of Catan* to the games that attempt historical recreation of factual colonization campaigns, like *Puerto Rico* (Borit, Borit, and Olsen 2018, 1–40). Many games, especially from the Eurogames lineage, are bound tightly to legacy traditions of play that emphasize resource acquisition, territorial expansion, and eradication of the enemies of progress. At her talk at the Canadian Games Studies Conference in 2022, Meghna Jayanth claimed that physical and digital games like these exist in the Imperial Mode, which she defined as:

> Games where enemies are killed, subjugated, displaced ... god games, turn-based military simulations, even farming games where the player dominates and brings to productive order the landscape ... games that are about conquest, war, overcoming enemies through violence, overthrowing nations, becoming king/boss/tycoon, or even achieving mastery over the game's systems.
>
> (Jayanth 2022)

A key question Jayanth asked in her talk at CGSA was why the game industries "bend so deeply toward designing worlds which tremble at the passage of the player", meaning worlds that acquiesce to their own domination and exploitation in the name of providing a rich power fantasy for players. Many colonization games allow competing players to carve up a map's natural resources through war or cultural domination, with the only question to resolve being which player colonizes the best. Of course, as scholars have continued to point out and identify the troubling implications of reifying colonial power fantasies for young players in a world that increasingly pursues a postcolonial future, board game players, hobbyists, and even mainstream media have begun to take notice of the ideology underpinning our games (Winkie 2021). It was in this environment that R. Eric Reuss first conceived of *Spirit Island*. In a developer's diary, Reuss described his game's origin story:

> There was a moment during a colonization action (of which game I can no longer recall: *Goa? Navegador? Endeavor?*) where my focus on the game elements cracked and fell away, replaced by the thought, "I wonder how ticked off the locals are about this new colony of foreigners. Well, we'll never know because this game has entirely abstracted away the people who already lived there. That's rude." Maybe I shared the thought, maybe people laughed, and we got back to the game.
>
> (Reuss, November 6, 2017)

All three titles he mentions are typical colonial games in the Eurogames tradition. *Goa*, as its name suggests, uses India as a backdrop for a game of European colonial spice trading and mercantile traffic. *Navegador* is a game of ocean colonization and trade focused on the Portuguese age of exploration. *Endeavor* is similar but swaps the Portuguese expansionists for factions throughout Europe and the Mediterranean. That Reuss cannot recall which of these games he was playing at the time should indicate just how common these themes and tropes are for serious board game hobbyists, and why he couldn't shake the idea that a game should be made that inverted the paradigm and placed the emphasis back on the land being conquered and the people most affected.

Reuss's interest in the land and peoples under colonial assault resulted in *Spirit Island,* which bills itself as a "Cooperative Settler-Destruction Strategy Game". In the game, players build the titular land mass from a set of modular board pieces depicting zones categorized by terrain type, including at least one coastal region. During setup, the players each choose a supernatural spirit whose power they will use to defend the island from colonist invaders. The invaders appear as white plastic tokens of three types: explorers, towns, and cities. Nobody plays the invaders; the invader actions are all determined by a deck of cards and a relentless turn order that mimics the colonial exploitation of land—first they explore into a zone, then they build permanent establishments, and then they pollute and corrupt the land through blight. The players, as spirits, must act quickly to dull the actions of the invaders, as blight has the effect of eradicating the "presence" of spirits in the various zones, represented by colored tokens that help to power the mystical abilities of the spirits and increase their destructive force. Each spirit is tightly themed and distinct. Vital Strength of the Earth is depicted in the game's art as a towering humanoid made of soil and stone. Consequently, the spirit is known to build slowly during play, initially weak and eventually devastating as its reach and power increases. By contrast Lightning's Swift Strike, a bird spirit constituted by lightning, is capable of heavy offense from its opening turns, but can do nothing to defend or heal the land. Solo play in *Spirit Island* is challenging for these reasons, and up to four players may choose spirits that complement one another and openly discuss strategy as they act simultaneously.

The invaders and spirits are not alone on the island. Honoring his initial critique of colonization games, Reuss included a fictional group of indigenous natives called the Dahan. Represented by tokens on the board resembling huts, the Dahan fight back when attacked by invaders but are no match for entrenched towns or cities. Therefore, the Dahan rely on the spirits to bolster them, move them, or protect them from the invaders that march across the terrain and blight the land.

Players lose the game if the island is too blighted by invader actions, if a spirit is destroyed completely via the loss of its presence tokens on the board, or if the invader deck exhausts. However, in an interesting twist, the conditions for victory get easier as play progresses. As the spirits act against invaders, they generate a resource called fear. In the early stage of the game, the spirits only win via complete eradication of the invaders, removing every invader piece from the board through the strategic use of their magical powers and resistance from the Dahan. As the spirits generate more and more fear, that condition is withdrawn and the players can win by razing all towns and cities, and eventually by just destroying the cities. Most successful *Spirit Island* sessions conclude this way, with many invader tokens remaining on the board.

The appeal of *Spirit Island*—both for players and the stakeholders for its market position—is in Reuss's counterfactual proposal. The game doesn't abandon the power fantasies that Jayanth laments. Instead, the game aims to invert them and grant the player incredible power to stomp out colonialist expansion with the resources and cultures available to the colonized as the invaders arrive. Rather than resist colonialist power fantasies, the game attempts to harness them in reverse and grant power to the colonized. The first words in the game's instruction manual clearly stage that fantasy: "You are powerful Spirits of the natural world, existing on an isolated island .... The Spirits of the Island must grow in power and throw back the invaders before the Island is blighted beyond hope of recovery!" (*Spirit Island* 2017, 3).

The Ludo-Textuality of Anti-Colonialist Play

Paul Booth describes the ludo-textual as a "way of analyzing the interaction between players and material elements within board games" (Booth 2021, 10–11). It is not enough, in other words, to analyze the textual components of a board game, or even the designed systems and mechanics of play. Other fields of media study from literature to film to digital content have benefited from innovating and utilizing textual analysis as a methodological tool, but Booth argues that identifying a board game's text is impossible without including in any analysis how the game is received and brought into being as an object of play. More so than many other media available for textual analysis, board games are use objects: meant to be touched, handled, manipulated, and altered. It is only through active perception and attention that board games fully actualize into readable texts, and therefore any analysis is incomplete without an account of how the game is played through actual sessions. This analysis of *Spirit Island* aggregates observations from over 20 sessions, from the perspective of a player and an observer, and includes plays with different groups of varying demographics, including play sessions found in online "Let's Play" videos. Through play, the patterns of use and ludological involvement with the game components reveal an intriguing, if troubled, relationship to colonialism.

Before proceeding it should be established and emphasized that *Spirit Island*, by all accounts, was designed in meticulous good faith as a true postcolonial board game experience with anti-colonial themes. Reuss carefully designed a satisfying gameplay experience through thoughtful inversion of the core elements of traditional settler Eurogames (Reuss, November 6, 2017). The central issue, observation of playthroughs suggest, is whether it is advisable or even plausible to use the tools of colonialist simulation to subvert or upend structures of the same.

Ludo-textual analysis begins with the game components and textual material. What is quickly apparent through examination is that *Spirit Island* does not represent any one specific colonial scenario so much as it represents the meta-reality of expansionist settlement itself, a broad concept of colonialism that abstracts the complexities of actual colonizing practice for one that can stand in for all exploration age expansion at once. The invaders are generic constructions. The plastic explorer figurines could represent Spaniards with morion helmets typically associated with conquistadors, but a search through the game's artwork on the various power cards reveals images of invaders in a mix of uniform colors, facial hair styles, and equipment that muddles their origin. One seeming exception is the game's concept of "adversaries", an advanced play addition that pits the spirits against specific and named historical enemies (England, Sweden, and Brandenburg-Prussia). But the rulebook suggests that even that nod to historical reality should not be read too literally: "Though the Adversaries may seem familiar, upon closer inspection you will find that the

Explorers of Spirit Island have a slightly different story to tell than your history books" (*Spirit Island* 2017, 26). Indeed dates, strategies, tactics, uniforms, and technology all fail to definitively identify a likely inspiration for the invaders, suggesting that the invaders are stand-ins for the concept of settler colonialism itself, which is among the most virulent and violent forms of colonial activity. Settler colonialism "is a distinct form of colonization in that its focus is on eliminating the indigenous in order to gain access to their land, as opposed to the focus of traditional colonialism on the extraction of resources—both natural and human, in the form of slaves" (Euteneuer 2018, 4–5). Since the invader actions inevitably result in the destruction of the Dahan and the extension of permanent settlements by the invaders, it is fair to suggest that this is a form of colonization the island faces. That necessarily means that *Spirit Island*, by opting for the arch villainy of settler colonialism, cannot depict the complex tools that historical colonists used to divide and dominate terrain, from mercantile exploitation, cultural absorption and appropriation, placing native populations into competition for resources, etc. On the island, the simplest form of colonialism is underway, leading to the clearest of stakes: as spirits, wipe out the invaders before they kill your followers.

Although described more specifically and with a greater expression of respectful detail, the Dahan are just as placeless as their invader enemies. The island terrain, Dahan dwellings, and spirit depictions evoke a vague sense of Pacific island heritage, but the truth is that the Dahan were intentionally designed to evoke no particular place or culture at all in a good faith attempt to avoid tokenizing and appropriating an actual culture, or trivializing a traumatic history for a colonized people. Even the Dahan's name was the subject of at least one week's research, according to Reuss (Chick 2017), to find a word constructed from near-universal phonemes that did not refer to or borrow vulgarity from any one culture. Although the manual identifies the game's time as the year 1700 A.D. (*Spirit Island* 2017, 26), there is no colonized territory at that time of interest to all three of the named adversaries that might provide a more definitive fix. The invaders, the Dahan, the spirits, and the island all draw from myriad historical and factual threads to weave an ahistorical and counterfactual "revenge" scenario for all colonized peoples against all colonizers, everywhere.

The generic meta-narrative of colonization is represented on the board symbolically by the very material of the game's tokens, confirmed by Reuss (Chick 2017). *Spirit Island* boards crowd with tokens during play as invaders and blight accumulate amidst Dahan huts and spirit presence. Tokens representing invaders or their blight are plastic sculpts, while the player's pieces and Dahan are made from wood or cardboard—tokens allegedly closer to the natural, and environmentally friendly. A successful playthrough of *Spirit Island*, then, has players confront a growing and expanding (mostly white, not accidentally) plastic menagerie and fight back with "natural" materials. By the end, there is more wood and cardboard then plastic on the board, a material victory for the island and a satisfying swap for players.

Representations of Exploitation

Spirit Island is thoughtful and well-meaning in its approach and construction of counterfactual power fantasies, which is why it was initially surprising to find that observations of play do not support the game's claims to anti-colonial discourse. Instead, play reveals that *Spirit Island* encourages players to reenact some destructive colonial practices, albeit with "good" or "noble" motives. This is most clear in the game's utilization of the Dahan.

Even Reuss laments his own choice to leave the Dahan as a nonplayable faction on the board without agency of their own. In interviews, Reuss has talked often about his desire to revisit the Dahan for a future expansion (Reuss 2018), as he is aware of the troubling implications of creating a colonized people in an anti-colonialist game and providing them no agency of their own. As Suckling has written elsewhere in this book, agency for the representations of the colonized in games—preferably at "strategic-level" (Suckling 2023, 3)—is a critical design element for successful postcolonial game mechanics. Suckling, citing Young, notes that it is the reclamation of agency by colonized cultures that allowed discourse of the postcolonial to begin (Suckling 2023, 2–3). By that account, *Spirit Island* immediately falls short of postcolonialism by relegating the Dahan to passive or reactionary roles—or worse. During play the Dahan do not move on their own, and only fight back when the invaders strike first. Additionally, players must master an essential mechanic of "pushing" and "gathering" Dahan for various beneficial effect. For example, spirits can push Dahan into territories soon to be attacked by explorers, knowing that the Dahan will strike back and kill the explorer. The spirit can therefore gather Dahan into a central zone to mount impressive defenses. Some powers even destroy the Dahan as readily as they do invaders, such as Swallow the Land-Dwellers, a power that simulates a massive tidal wave pulling invaders and Dahan alike into the sea. The Dahan sacrifice becomes collateral damage in the larger fight, necessary for the greater good of winning. During observation, some players commented on feeling uncomfortable with the thematic unwilling sacrifice of the Dahan to the spirits' whims, an example of what Booth describes as a tendency of colonialist games to force players into situations in which they are "complicit in culturally insensitive ways" (Booth 2021, 179). More troubling, however, most players observed rationalized the implied sacrifices as just another game mechanic. The Dahan ceased to be meta-representations of colonized peoples and transformed instead to object resources that performed useful functions at strategic moments. Players developed strategies about methods and timing for maneuvering the Dahan–just another token on the board.

Reuss addresses the Dahan's lack of agency in the game's lore, describing how the Dahan's relative weakness is a result of the invaders having ravaged them with disease just prior to the events of the game. Also, the Dahan are described as being "divided" in their opinion on how to handle the colonists as some Dahan are "fascinated with their lifestyle, tools, and beliefs" (*Spirit Island* 2017, 24). Dahan ambivalence in the face of extinctive settler colonialism, even if beset with an illness caused by invasion, places the Dahan into a problematic role that Mukherjee identifies with the subaltern. In a game inspired by the lack of a colonized perspective in popular colonization games, *Spirit Island* relegates the Dahan to an othered position in which they *lack* structure, organization, and inspiration with which to protect their own lives and homes. As Mukherjee notes, colonialist ideology—often emergent in the colonialist Eurogames Reuss used as his inspiration—often presumes that the colonized "can only achieve chaos" without the aid of the colonizers, placing the colonized into what Fanon calls the "zone of nonbeing" from which the colonized are never fully elevated to the status of full human beings (Mukherjee 2017, 65–66). Rather than frame the game around, at minimum, defense of the Dahan, *Spirit Island* organizes a competition between the invaders and the spirits/players that asks whether the spirits can successfully exploit the Dahan resource before the invaders can extract it, pitting the players and the game into a battle reminiscent of the Eurogames that inspired *Spirit Island* in the first place—who can be the *best* at using colonist tactics to achieve game goals? In fact, the Dahan are so expendable that players don't need them to win. Victory instead relies on managing the population of explorers and towns—a metaphor for assimilation. The spirits/players triumph by holding the invaders in check, while Dahan survival is irrelevant.

Reuss recognized the problems with the message that the Dahan communicate and claims that during development he deeply entertained the idea of abandoning the spirits to reimagine the game as a Dahan rebellion story, but conceded that industrial concerns forced him back to his original idea, as "changes would have removed many of the things testers had said they particularly enjoyed about the game" (Reuss, July 23, 2017), meaning that the game was much more desirable as a published title with the spirit theme intact. As a media text, *Spirit Island* is more valuable as a commodified narrative appealing to postcolonial players (Linder 2016, 197–214) with familiar, comforting game mechanics. This means *Spirit Island* fits within Jayanth's inventory of power fantasy tropes, emerging as a game about land and resources in thrall to the player. Invaders and spirits compete over board spaces via blight and presence, creating a tension about who occupies what land, and which side can take the best advantage of the map. When considering this in tandem with the empty agency of the Dahan, the anti-colonial stance of *Spirit Island* exists almost entirely within the theme, not within the experience of play itself. One could swap the spirits for, say, an opposing colonial army and the battle for land and power would remain nearly the same.

Taking this thought further, one observed group of players briefly commented on how the invaders appeared to function as anti-spirits. The invaders do not wield magical powers; they expand and ravage on predictable rotations. The *effect*, however, shares similarities with the spirits. Invaders leave their own kind of presence as blight, which cascades into adjacent territories and expands the scope of their influence. The coasts cannot be blocked, guaranteeing an endless and renewable supply of reinforcements, granting them a kind of immortality without spirit aid. Against the near-helpless Dahan, the invaders are mythic, as they have power enough to challenge the spirits, making *Spirit Island* effectively a struggle between two godlike powers. For an anti-colonialist game, this hews uncomfortably close to the exploration narrative of white godhood, in which native peoples submitted and supplicated in the face of the pristine and divine beings who arrived on their shores, a narrative that has been rightfully complicated and debunked to various degrees in recent years (Subin 2022). A playthrough of *Spirit Island* has the tendency to reaffirm the abstraction of the colonized in favor of a classical, familiar playthrough of colonialist competition for land, people, and pyrrhic victory, turning counter-factuality into a tool that reaffirms the dominant colonialist ideology, as Mukherjee has observed in many counterfactual games (Mukherjee 2017, 75–99). These choices may have made the game more accessible and palatable to a generation of board game hobbyists who are familiar with Eurogame mechanics but do not want to reenact historical atrocities. As Apperley has suggested, a substantial gaming community gains pleasure from engaging with familiar game mechanics in counterfactual scenarios (Apperley 2018, 1–22), which provided *Spirit Island* with an enthusiastic player base hungry for its ahistorical themes while the game continued to traffic in tropes it sought to upend.

Ahistorical Games and Asymmetrical Design

Much has been written in this volume on the ways in which historical games can function as heritage, which Mochocki has defined as the ways in which history is *used* in cultural practice (Mochocki 2021, 1–23). But, of course, board games also have their own history, a history that has relied heavily on abstracting and gamifying destructive ideologies to portray historical scenarios as they supposedly were. One possible reading of *Spirit Island*—perhaps an unorthodox one—is that the game uses the history *of board games* as heritage, deploying the superstructure of the long history of gameplay mechanics and iteration in the colonialist tradition to dismantle the tradition from the inside. If so, observations of gameplay of *Spirit Island* do not suggest that the experiment succeeded. Players overwhelmingly praise the game's design precisely because it is an exemplary version of the types of games hobbyists enjoy, the games that form a core legacy of the form. As play opens, they possess territory in a limited sense via their presence tokens, they seek expansion to increase their power, they utilize resources that include the native populations, and they win by eradicating an enemy force. *Spirit Island* presents players with a chance to right a historical wrong, but only arms and incentivizes them with colonial tactics to fight colonizers. To adopt the strategies of the colonizer, including the exploitation of the Dahan as a valuable and expendable resource, is the most privileged and rewarded path in *Spirit Island*, despite the game's seeming criticism of those tropes.

Conclusions

Earlier in the chapter came an assertion that researchers had to do more than simply identify problems in games, so this chapter concludes with suggestions for alternative paths anti-colonial games might explore in depicting anti-colonial scenarios of "settler-destruction" (or perhaps other games that might wish to dismantle mercantile capitalist expansion, exploration and resource extraction, and so on). One suggestion: designers should consider complementing ahistorical scenarios with asymmetrical design. *Spirit Island* is a game that uses colonization tactics to attack colonialism, and so the game's theme is overwhelmed by its ludic discourse (Booth 2021, 59). *Spirit Island* argues the tactics of settler colonialism are justified if the *cause* is just. Good motives are enough to launder cold calculation over resources and grasping for land if the enemy's motives are bad enough.

Instead, designers should feel emboldened to create games that dismantle the harmful practices of history that benefit from the colonialist heritage of board games. Imagine a game in the mold of *Spirit Island* that asks players to dismantle colonialism without participating in it. Perhaps players could face the threat of relentless colonialist exploitation armed with different tactics perhaps healing instead of harming, perhaps using magic and power to support and bolster the colonized out of their downtrodden state until they can defend themselves, blunting and blocking the attack of the invaders until there is no more value in expanding. Or, perhaps, a system based around preserving and entrenching culture to resist assimilation and erasure. The specifics should be left to talented designers who, moving beyond the heritage of colonialist design, can explore what it means to leave the colonialist design in the past, for good.

References

Apperley, Tom. 2018. "Counterfactual Communities: Strategy Games, Paratexts and the Player's Experience of History." *Open Library of Humanities* 4, no. 1: 15. https:// olh.openlibhums.org/article/id/4472/
Bogost, Ian. 2010. *Persuasive Games.* Cambridge, MA: MIT Press.
Booth, Paul. 2021. *Board Games as Media.* New York, NY: Bloomsbury Academic.
Borit, Cornel, Melania Borit, and Petter Olsen. 2018. "Representations of Colonialsim in Three Popular Modern Board Games: *Puerto Rico, Struggle of Empires,* and *Archipelago.*" *Open Library of Humanities* 4, no. 1: 17, 1–40. https://doi.org/ 10.16995/olh.211

Chapman, Adam, Anna Foka, and Jonathan Westin. 2017. "Introduction: What is Historical Game Studies?" *Rethinking History* 21, no. 3: 358–371. https://doi.org/10.1080/13642529.2016.1256638

Chick, Tom. 2017. "R. Eric Reuss and Spirit Island." *Quarter to Three*, podcast audio, September 7, 2017. https://www.quartertothree.com/fp/2017/09/07/qt3-games-podcast-r-eric-reuss-spirit-island/

Euteneuer, Jacob. 2018. "Settler Colonialism in the Digital Age: *Clash of Clans*, Territoriality, and the Erasure of the Native." *Open Library of Humanities* 4, no. 1: 14, 1–24. https://doi.org/10.16995/olh.212

Jayanth, Meghna. 2022. "Game Design in the Imperial Mode #CGSA 2022." Medium. com. https://medium.com/@betterthemask/game-design-in-the-imperial-mode-cgsa-2022-e5a9a6a57859

Jayemanne, Darshana. 2018. *Performativity in Art, Literature, and Videogames*. Cham: Springer.

Linder, Oliver. 2016. "Commodification." *Postcolonial Studies Meets Media Studies*. 197–214. Bielefeld: Transcript printing.

Mochocki, Michal. 2021. *Role-play as a Heritage Practice*. London: Routledge.

Mukherjee, Souvik. 2017. *Videogames and Postcolonialism: Empire Plays Back*. Cham: Palgrave Macmillan.

Murray, Soraya. 2018. "The Work of Postcolonial Game Studies in the Play of Culture." *Open Library of Humanities* 4, no. 1: 13, 1–25. https://doi.org/10.16995/olh.285

Peterson, Jon. 2012. *Playing at the World*. San Diego, CA: Unreason Press.

Reddit. 2020. "Anti-capitalist and anti-colonial games." r/boardgames. Last modified 2020. https://www.reddit.com/r/boardgames/comments/l0tz6b/anticapitalist_and_anticolonial_games/

Reuss, R. Eric. 2018. "AMA." r/boardgames. Last modified October 2018. https://www.reddit.com/r/boardgames/comments/9rb66x/im_r_eric_reuss_designer_of_spirit_island_ama/

Reuss, R. Eric. July 23, 2017. "*Spirit Island* Design Diary – The Dahan." Boardgamegeek. com. https://boardgamegeek.com/blogpost/67292/spirit-island-design-diary-dahan

Reuss, R. Eric. November 6, 2017. "Designer Diary: *Spirit Island*, or Inverting the Colonization Trope." Boardgamegeek.com. https://boardgamegeek.com/blogpost/67955/designer-diary-spirit-island-or-inverting-coloniza

Reynolds, Daniel. 2019. *Media in Mind*. New York, NY: Oxford.

Subin, Anna Della. 2022. "How to Kill a God: The Myth of Captain Cook Shows How the Heroes of Empire Will Fall." The Guardian. https://www.theguardian.com/news/2022/jan/18/how-to-kill-a-god-captain-cook-myth-shows-how-heroes-of-empire-will-fall

Suckling, Maurice. 2023. "Design Elements in Postcolonial Commercial Historical Board Wargames." In this volume.

Winkie, Luke. 2021. "The Board Games That Ask You to Reenact Colonialism." The Atlantic. https://www.theatlantic.com/culture/archive/2021/07/board-games-have-colonialism-problem/619518/

5 Unearthing Ancient Roots? Recognizing and Redefining Mexican Identity through Board Games

Miguel Angel Bastarrachea Magnani

Introduction

In this chapter, I will attempt to problematize board gaming culture in Mexico by unveiling the formation of Mexican identity, a direct result of colonization, and next by discussing the state of the art of the Mexican board gaming community and its challenges. The study of postcolonial features in games is not restricted, however, to those games that explicitly deal with mechanics and themes related to postcolonialism (like conquest, dominance, and the exploitation of resources). As Mukherjee explains, postcolonial "does not simply mean 'after colonialism'", the end of colonialism, or even solely address scenarios in formerly colonized countries after their independence. The development of new elites within neocolonial institutions in post-independence societies has perpetuated similar complaints of unequal treatment and exploitation" (Mukherjee, 2017, 3). In the Mexican case, the onset of new elites in postcolonial societies will be central as we will see. According to Booth, game themes are "one way of observing how different cultural anxieties or passions manifest" (2021, 167). Thus, at the end of the chapter, I will pay attention to Mexican board games whose theme is related to pre-Hispanic, precolonial heritage. Investigating board game culture in Contemporary Mexico is timely not only due to the recent interest in postcolonial gaming (Mukherjee and Hammar, 2018) and how it allows engaging with cultural heritage (Mochocki, 2021) but also because of the few studies that have focused on the topic.

Disentangling Mexican Identity

Understanding Mexican identity has been a significant issue for the Mexican people even before its inception as an independent nation at the start of the nineteenth century (López and Zagal, 1998; Uranga, 2013). Mexicans often look only at their pre-Hispanic roots in a desperate quest to find an identity. However, the identity is bound to the encounter between the Hispanic Empire and the precolonial cultures. Hence, there are two sources from which Mexican heritage draws: the Mesoamerican lineage constituted from a diversity

DOI: 10.4324/9781003356318-5

of cultures active during the conquest (Mexica, Mayan, Purépecha, Mixtec, among many others) and from the *Criollos* (creoles), i.e., people from the New World whose two parents were born in Peninsular Spain.

From 1521 to 1821, the territory that we nowadays call Mexico was known as the Viceroyalty of New Spain, at some point including part of Central America and several southern US states. New Spain originated from the conquest of Mexico-Tenochtitlan by Hernán Cortés in 1521 and was officially established as a territorial entity of the Spanish Empire in 1535. The Viceroyalty was abolished in 1820 in favor of Mexico as an independent nation. After dominating the Mexicas (traditionally known as the Aztecs) and making pacts with their enemies like the Tlaxcaltecs, the conquerors established themselves in *encomiendas*. These labor systems were given to them as their reward. Using them, they took advantage of the wealth that the New World offered for the Empire.

Culturally speaking, the *novohispano* (the demonym of New Spain) period is Mexico's colonial period. It goes mainly from the arrival of the evangelizers around 1525 to the independence of New Spain in 1821. During this time, a well-structured system of racial hierarchies was maintained, made up of the *Peninsulares* (those born in peninsular Spain), *Criollos*, *Mestizos* (scions of Spanish and Native Americans), and other castes, and finally, the indigenous (the original inhabitants of the New World), who were at the bottom of the ladder (García Saiz, 1989). The *Peninsulares* held the most important political and economic positions, displacing the *Criollos* even though they were the ones who could call New Spain their home. On the other hand, the castes and indigenous people could hardly access a position of importance.

New Spain was not considered a colony of the Empire as such. The colony concept would arise later under the dynamics of British imperialism. The Spanish Empire intended to construct a copy of the "metropolis" model for New Spain. In other words, the Spanish Viceroyalties were supposed to be replicas of Spain, historically European and geographically American (O'Gorman, 1970). From the point of view of the *Criollos*, hence, New Spain was another province, so they should deserve the same political and economic opportunities as the *Peninsulares*. In practice, this was not true, giving rise to discontent and resentment among the *Criollo* population. The *Peninsulares* had no attachment to the New World, even when it was the source of their wealth, and they shamelessly supported each other in prejudice against the *Criollos*. So, *Criollos* only found the need to build an identity to face the *Peninsulares*. This identity is called *criollismo* or *novohispanidad* (*New-Spanishness*). We emphasize that mestizos were gradually incorporated into this identity, as they met the cultural requirements to some extent. This was not the case for Native Americans and most of the castes who were put aside from this representation.

The Three Foundational Myths

The *Criollo*'s conscience was to know that they were the heirs of the conquerors, who had forged the Viceroyalty with their blood, only to see their right being taken away by the *Peninsulares*. The New Spanish *Criollos*, sons and daughters of Spanish, were no longer Spanish, but neither were they Mexicans. Therefore, *Criollos* resorted to three axes around which they forged *novohispanidad*. These "*Criollo* myths" were religion, the pre-Hispanic past, and the wealth of the New World (Aspe Armella, 2002). Religion was inherited directly from the Spanish Empire. Catholicism defined and constituted the Spanish monarchy, which was considered a defender of the faith. In fact, the implantation of the faith was an argument for the Spanish Crown's legitimacy for the conquest and custody of its territories in America. However, faith was not enough. An extra ingredient was necessary to carve a Criollo Catholicism: the rescue of the pre-Hispanic past.

Despite the indigenous people being the original inhabitants of the New World, *Criollos*, and later *Mestizos*, had to feel proud of the indigenous past of New Spain. Highlighting pre-Hispanic cultures was to affirm a trait of their own that the *Peninsulares* did not share. The Spanish Empire was concerned about the status of the indigenous people in the mid-sixteenth century. A discussion arose on the legitimacy of the dispossession and exploitation they had suffered since the conquest: the Valladolid debate led by Juan Ginés de Sepúlveda and Bartolomé de las Casas (de Sepúlveda, 1975). A specific defense of the conquered had to be accepted, with which the *Criollos* affirmed themselves.

Of course, this defense would be superficial because it would lead to indigenism and paternalism over the years. This brought explicit contradictions: defending the indigenous past was to excuse idolatry, but accepting the truth of Catholicism implied the demonization and rejection of the pre-Hispanic past. Faced with the impossibility of uprooting idolatry, *Criollos* forged a new religion on it. The primary example is the inculturation of Catholicism in the Virgin of Guadalupe figure, which finally gave them a trump card. Guadalupanism became a distinctive trait of Mexican Catholicism. A brown virgin, a Mexican virgin. This inculturation brought to the secular domain would be a signature of Mexican heritage.

The last pillar of *criollismo* was the exaltation of natural resources of the New World. The *novohispano* was proud of the natural beauties, the cities, the landscape, the land, and the wealth. *Criollos* used to compare the benefits of America against the European landscape lacking such prodigality. It was an affirmation of the ability of the *Criollo* to live up to the *Peninsular* and the rest of the world by having a vast land full of resources, exotic, fertile, and without equal. The extravagance of altarpieces (*retablos*) in Mexican churches, for example, is a proclamation of the plenitude and benefits of the New World.

A World of Contradictions

The people of New Spain lived in a world of opposites, dilemmas, contradictions, and absurdities, just like Mexico today. *Criollo* had to express this tension, and it did so through a particular kind of temperament of the spirit: the *barroco* (baroque), the peak of the formation of the *Criollo* identity. Baroque is considered a cultural, artistic movement that spanned Western history between the seventeenth and eighteenth centuries (Bustillo, 1988). Baroque art was the instrument by which the *Criollos* achieved a transfiguration of his sensitive being: in architecture, through the penumbra of spaces; in literature, through the obscurity of metaphors; in philosophy, through dilemmas and aporias (Bustillo, 1988). Baroque allowed *Criollos* to create an apology for everything American in New Spain, so it was more than an artistic movement but also an intellectual, cultural, and philosophical one at the roots of the *novohispanidad*.

Barroco subsists thanks to the differences instead of annihilating them. It is unifying but not homogenizing; identity is achieved through alterity and opposition. It is dynamic, violent, eccentric, fiery, and dark: an explosion of subjectivity exalting movement (López Farjeat and Zagal Arreguín, 1998). In a baroque unit, the absurd lives and coexists at ease, and the opposites mix and integrate. Without contrast, there is no meaning. The Mexican universe, so complex since the conquest – and perhaps even before – finds an expression of its constant change and maturation in the *barroco*.

It should be noted that Spain was already a contradictory entity by the sixteenth century. It was a medieval empire, defender of the Faith, rejecting the idea of progress regulating the rest of the Western world. Simultaneously, they carried out "Renaissance activities" such as discovery and conquest. *Criollos* inherited these contradictions and shaped them in the New World. Criollo synthesis necessary to deal with the conflict at the heart of New Spain would be possible only under a baroque temperament able to assume all those cultural tensions and aporias. Baroque stood as a criterion of significance and the condition of possibility for the persistence of heterogeneity against colonial homogenization:

> It is said that in the so-called Callejón de la Condesa in Mexico City (…), two luxurious carriages met face to face. Since the two could not pass due to the narrowness, the drivers mutually ordered each other to give way to their masters. But neither of them wanted to give way: they were nobles. Realizing that, in addition, the two travelers were of the same lineage and ancestry, the matter was complicated. Giving way to the other was equivalent to acknowledging the superiority of the other. Both carriages were parked for days. The lackeys served food to their masters in their carriages, both determined not to let the

other pass. The matter came into the hands of the viceroy, whom solomonically ordered both carriages to move backward simultaneously. So, no one was offended.

(López Farjeat and Zagal Arreguín, 1998, 47, translation mine)

Contrary to the standard – enlightened and rational – approach of Western society, the dynamics of a baroque society are settled down in action: there are no pre-established hierarchies.

Life Is a Dream

Barroco is predominantly metaphorical (Deleuze, 1992). Metaphors are its way of expressing itself, as they integrate contradictions by establishing analogies, going beyond being an alternative resource to rational processes. As long as *barroco* is metaphorical, it is sensual and employs images as a resource. The mythical, magic, and poetic appeals to universal validity through something particular and concrete. The language of myths flourishes, and entities undergo trans-substantiation: a synthesis of philosophy and poetry emerges as in Sor Juana Inés de la Cruz's poem *Primero Sueño* (*First Dream*) (Aspe Armella, 2002; de la Cruz, 2006). *barroco* revealed to the *Criollos* what their society was and wanted to be, offering a fundamentally aesthetic way of existing by building a mythical world. *Criollos* were eager for this environment because they needed to show their worth to the world, which could be achieved through power and recognition, and baroque facilitates boasting, pomp, appearance, and magnificence (López Farjeat and Zagal Arreguín, 1998).

On the other hand, although not much is known about the rationality of Mesoamerican people, it has been considered that Nahuatl (the language of the Mexica) was also poetic (Aspe Armella, 2002). It would have consisted of sensual categories different from conceptual ones and closer to metaphorical ones. Essential relationships of things would have been established from analogies, as exhibited in the codices. Nahuatl thought would then be one that neither affirms nor denies, a thought in which opposites coexist and are integrated, where the contradiction of the concrete reality that it indicates is assumed. For some, the *barroco* of the Americas would have already been there in the aesthetics and culture of pre-Hispanic peoples. However, one must be careful not to fall into the "good savage" colonial discourse. The truth is that little is known about pre-Hispanic thought.

The Identity of Contemporary Mexico

Criollos were the inheritors of colonial institutions, which would later be left to the *mestizos*. The passage from the New Spain *Criollo* to the Mexican of today is marked by the social, political, and cultural movements of the XIX,

XX, and XXI centuries, and above all, by the emergence of the *Mestizo*, which is Spanish, indigenous, and neither. Despite the modern, pejorative dimension of the concept, Mexico is a result of miscegenation. Initially, the *Mestizo* was a specific caste, the scion of a *Peninsular* male and an indigenous woman; however, with time, it began to denote all the other castes (descendants of Spanish, Native Americans, African Mexican Americans, and so on). If the New Spanish *Criollo* lived in the contradiction of being and not being Spanish, the tension would become stronger in the Mestizo. Unsurprisingly, in such an ambiguous situation, the postcolonial *Mestizo* took the baroque identity and made the Criollo myths their own once the *Criollo* had disappeared. Thus, if the *Criollo* was baroque by necessity, the Mexican is baroque by an original condition. Hence, we Mexicans live in a mythical world, even if we are unaware of it. Guadalupanism is still a pillar of national identity and *indigenism* part of our speech. We still need the glitz and pomp to assert ourselves against the rest of the world. The bragging is manifest, just as outrageous: it is enough to see antennas, the private television signal covering an endless number of tin roofs. We are still *Criollos*, although not in New Spain anymore.

One hundred years after the start of Mexico's independence movement, the postcolonial country was shaped by the 30 years known as the *Porfiriato*. The dictator Porfirio Díaz ruled the country from 1876 to 1910, when he was deposed by the Mexican Revolution (Schlarman, 1950). The central axis during this period was to modernize the country, to establish the idea of progress from the point of view of positivism. Adopting these trends confronted the identity that the *Criollo* had forged (O'Gorman, 1970). Porfirio Díaz fostered a colonial process by adopting features of French culture for Mexico's modernization.

Unfortunately, in a large part of Western thought, the extravagance and magnificence of the baroque have been considered unnecessary, ridiculous, incomprehensible, imperfect, overloaded, scandalous, pathological, monstrous, or in bad taste. These unfounded ideas came from their clash against the Enlightenment and the aesthetics of Classicism. Under the aegis of progress, enlightened rationalism asserts the functional and utilitarian, striving for a society where people are equal, molded through citizenship, equal rights, and positivism (Berlin, 2013). By promising constancy and regularity, enlightened rationalism denies the extraordinary and the miraculous, thus stripping the mythical and the metaphorical of any possibility as a form of expression. Therefore, *barroco* was rejected, caricatured, and marginalized from Mexico as an independent nation, which was equivalent to confronting the very nature of our identity. Rejecting the amalgamation, where the absurd and otherness manifest daily, caused an unnecessary delay in Mexico's cultural maturation. In other words, by denying *barroco* in pursuit of Western modernity, Mexicans denied themselves.

Mexican being is accidental because, in the face of the *substance,* it is *nothing*, but it is *being* in the face of *nothing* (Uranga, 2013). Hence,

Mexican society is like a tableau, an amalgamation of contradictory elements that affirm plurality and life, as the Mexican philosopher Samuel Ramos explains, "to build houses with slate mansard roofs, in the Parisian style, in the middle of Paseo de la Reforma, in Mexico City, as if there were snowfalls in these latitudes" (Ramos, 1951, 49, translation mine). We can observe Mexican *barroco* in countless examples: in the typical dishes and candies of the different regions of the country, the *mole,* to name a few, made of chocolate and *chile*, integrating elements that we would commonly think contradictory, sweet and salty, pre-Hispanic and Spanish. Of course, also in board games.

Traditional Board Games

The presence of adult games is known in Mesoamerica. It is said that "Hernán Cortés and Pedro de Alvarado came to play *totolli* or *totoloqui* with Moctezuma while they held him prisoner. The *totolli* was a game like bowling that the ancient Mexicans practiced and that, according to Bernal Díaz del Castillo, belonging to Moctezuma, had all its pieces made of gold" (González y González et al., 1993, 49, translation mine). However, it was in New Spain that entertainment became a commodity within the *Criollo* society. The *novohispanos* had many entertainment activities, primarily public spectacles and competencies connected to the religious calendar and holidays. Card games were also played during the colonial period, and by the beginning of the nineteenth century board games of French origin were already circulating (González y González et al., 1993).

Besides games like Domino, *Damas Chinas* (Chinese checkers), and Chess, some traditional board games in Mexico are important as they reflect cultural motifs. Among them, one finds *Lotería* (Lottery), *Serpientes y Escaleras* (Serpents and Snakes), *El Juego de la Oca* (The Goose Game), *el Coyote* (the Coyote), and *Corre qué te alcanzo* (Run that I'll catch you). Among them, the most representative of Mexican heritage is perhaps *Lotería*. The game is of European origin (it came from Italy in the fifteenth century) and arrived in Mexico around the nineteenth century (Ortiz Lanz, 2017). It is a board game of chance composed of 54 card-deck illustrations with symbolic motifs and a set of tables with the same images. It is played similarly to *Bingo*, where beans are placed over the tables every time one of the figures is drawn from the deck. The figures have changed throughout the decades. The most popular version was printed in 1887 by the French entrepreneur Clemente Jacques living in Mexico (the same persona that later founded the food processing company that bears his name) (Ortiz Lanz, 2017). In that deck, the first card is a rooster (for some, reminiscent of France). There are other popular versions, like the one created by the tradesman José María Evia in 1859 to promote his brand of cigarettes or the one printed by the Mexican illustrator José Guadalupe Posada at the beginning of the twentieth century (Masera Ceruti, 2017; Ortiz Lanz, 2017).

Later, after the Mexican Revolution, the figures in *Lotería* began to be recognized as motifs that speak about Mexican identity. Some characters were lost, like the cards of "Adam" and "Eve", or those of "*La Seductora*" (the seductress) and "*El Perverso*" (the pervert); the rest remain: "*El Diablo*" (the devil), "*La Muerte*" (the death), and "*La Sirena*" (the mermaid). *Lotería*'s iconography constitutes touchstones for Mexican cultural heritage, at least from the postcolonial era once the *Mestizos* replaced the *Criollos*. Mexican people took over *Lotería* from the upper classes to make their own cards and play them in religious and secular festivities. They embedded the game with both oral and visual traditions. For example, it is said that the "*La Calavera*" (the skull) card is an allegory of the *Día de Muertos* (Day of the Death), and "*La Chalupa*" (a small boat) represents the Xochimilcan Lake, a popular tourist destination in Mexico City that once was used by the Mexica for agricultural practices over artificial islands. On the other hand, several of the pictures in the *Lotería* are inadequate representations of minorities and preserve prejudices against them, like racial representations ["*El Negrito*" (the little black), "*El Apache*" (the apache)], gender representations ["*La Dama*" (the lady) and "*El Catrín*" (the gentleman)] or even addictions ["*El Borracho*" (the drunken)]. *Lotería* is so important to Mexican culture that it is usually reproduced with different themes and pictures, where there is an effort to remove deprecating representations. Its images transmit cultural values and create new meanings as didactic material for specific communities (Zapata Flores, 2010). There is a *Google Doodle* devoted to *Lotería* (https://www.google.com/doodles/celebrating-loteria?hl=es-419) if you want to peek a look. *Lotería* reflects the baroque sensuality of the Mexican spiritual framework and its capacity to generate new mythologies easily.

In 1963, *Novedades Montecarlo* (*Montecarlo Novelties*) was founded by Carmen Mercado and her sons (Enriquez Vázquez, 2021). For a long time, the company was the most popular for the board gaming community and family entertainment. Not only they distributed traditional games like *Lotería* and *Serpientes y Escaleras* and popular games like Chinese Checkers and Domino, but also, they brought to Mexico Spanish versions of American games. For example, the *Monopoly* game in Mexico is called *Turista Mundial* (*World Tourist*). There are mirror versions of several games like *Clue*, *¿Quién es el culpable?* (*Who is guilty?*), and so on. During the 1980s and 1990s, foreign companies gained terrain in the market and dominated it for several decades. Only recently have Mexican designers become increasingly interested in to making new games.

Contemporary Board Game Culture in Mexico

During the last two decades, Mexico has tried to catch up with recent trends, i.e., with Eurogames. *Eurogame* is a label assigned to a large variety of games characterized by being abstract, strategic, and with indirect participant interaction, contrary to the "American style" games that rely more upon luck (Woods, 2009). Their name reflects the trend emerging in Germany during the 1960s and 1970s. To date, there are around one hundred Mexican board games developed by independent Mexican publishers. A complete classification of board games in Mexico, or even a full list, would be challenging partly because most are self-published or still in development.

I follow the model proposed by Booth to analyze board games as a cultural phenomenon. Board game communities have a lower entry barrier than video games (Booth, 2021, 169). As a result, players quickly become designers and critics of games. Then, there would be four layers: (1) the board game players, (2) online content creators that play as intermediaries by reviewing and explaining games, (3) designers, and (4) companies. As it happens in other cultures, designers may be either employees of (more or less) consolidated companies, freelancers devoted professionally to the trade, or hobbyists who make games (that's why crowdfunding platforms are the obvious option to get support). Below, I will present a provisional recount of board games in Mexico, listing companies that have published two or more games. In this stage of Mexican board gaming, people are quickly shifting between gamers, reviewers, designers, and companies. Of course, this does not mean that a company that has published several games has gained more recognition; it depends on whether their games are *actually being played*. I apologize in advance for any omission.

At the beginning of the twenty-first century, the company *Ludika y Artefaktos* published the party game *Adigma* (Cortés, 2012a); ten years later, *Adidoku* (Cortés, 2012b), and 20 years later, *Rana Sapiens* (Cortés, 2022), which are puzzle-solving oriented. *Adidoku* has several themes, including a thematic one for Francisco Villa, an icon from Mexican Revolution. While *Adigma* and *Adidoku* are well-known family games, the Eurogames trend started in the 10s. One of the first euro "Mexican" games was *Cazadores de Fósiles* (Fossil Hunters) (Escalante and Escalante, 2011a) by Xiba Games, a game focused on resource administration in a paleontological setup. Xiba Games produced two games with Mesoamerican themes: *La tumba del Rey Pakal* (*King Pakal's Tomb*) (Escalante and Escalante, 2011b) and *Jardín botánico de Tehuacán* [*Botanical Garden of Tehuacán*] (Escalante and Escalante, 2013). From there, several independent companies started publishing Eurogames regularly. Among the more consolidated, i.e., those that have created three or more games, we find *Ludens Games*, a publisher from Jalisco who has made *Colorbugs* (Ramos, 2019b), *Antes del Diluvio* [*Before the Deluge*] (Sánchez, 2019), the party game *Folclore* (Ramos, 2019a), *Pájaros en el Alambre* [*Birds on the Wire*] (Ramos, 2020), *Fotozoo* (Benitez López, 2021), and *Rolling Farmers* (Calderón Espinoza, 2021). *Lighthouse Games* has created *Doxa: the card game* (Luzarreta, 2018), the roll and write game *Aban!* (Dzib, 2022a), *Hitodama* (Luzarreta, 2012), and *Bite and Treaty* (Suarez Olivares, 2022), which is in development. *Guerras Gato Games* have published

Guerras Gato [*Cat Wars*] (López Valdepeña, 2016b) and *Kanyimajo* (López Valdepeña, 2016a) and *Bakenero: Soul Reaper* (López Valdepeña, 2018). *Gnomosapiens* has created *Necronomicorp* (Escalante, 2016), *Card Game: The Card Game* (Escalante, 2019), *Backyard of Frutabaja* (Escalante, 2021a), funded by Kickstarter, and *Filler Clash* (Escalante, 2021b). *Arroyo Ibarra & Asociados* is another company from Metepec that creates strategic games like *Ollinkalli* (Arroyo, 2016). *Malinche Games makes* strategic games based on Mexican History, such as *Tierra y Libertad: Mexican Revolution* (Sanchez, 2018), *Timeline Revolution* (Sanchez, 2020), *Patria Libre* [Free Homeland] (Sanchez, 2022). *Detestable Games* is a game incubator that has published *Meeplepalooza* (Artigas and Jager, 2018), *Lords of Xibalba* (Esteva, 2018), *Seat Wars* (Ayala, 2018), *Cooks & Crooks* (Muñoz and Novelo, 2019), *Geisha* (Coronado, 2019), *Party Warriors* (Luna, 2019). *Draco Studio* is a publisher that made *Dragons of the Red Moon: The Gauntlet* (Hernández, 2019a), *Pátzcuaro* (Hernández, 2019b) and collaborated with *Gnomosapiens* and *Detestable Games* to create the popular game *Dodos Riding Dinos* (Hernández and Escalante, 2021) funded on *Kickstarter*, *Kiwi Show Down* (Macba and Escalante, 2022) with *Detestable Games* and *Board Zeppelin*, and is developing *Party Panda Pirates* (Alamo Borja et al., 2022).

There are other small companies still in the process of consolidation; such is the case of *Moneta Games* which is in the making of *All Fathers* (Rolón, 2022a), *Ts'Unu'Um* (Zamora, 2022), and *Eris: Seed of Discord* (Rolón, 2022b). Also, several indie games are self-published or produced by small single-game companies. Like *Infected: The Board Game* (Guizar, 2017), *Dark Maiden* (Luna, 2018), *TerrorXico* (Escalante Hernández, 2018), *Microcosmos* (Corza and Uribe, 2019), *Tattoo Brawl* (Whiu, 2019), *False God's Fall* (Armijo Castro, 2020), *Ofrendados* (Perez Tovar, 2021), *Gigamic* (Escalante and Escalante, 2021b), *Souvenirs* (Moya, 2021), *Las Mañas del Poder* [Tricks of Power] (Hernández, 2022), *Make a Boys Love Story* (Donovan et al., 2022), *Neuroriders* (Suarez Olivares and Giordano, 2022), *Toongeon Fights* (Fernandez, 2022), Card Games like *Yortuk* (Bayardo Dodge, 2016), *Tricksters* (Burgos and Ramos, 2016), *Chakkan: The Card Game* (Cabrera Fernández, 2019), *Weapon Wars* (Perez Tovar, 2019), *Chronicles of Marlis* (Mendez, 2021), *Cook King* (Gutman Duering, 2022), *Kaikoro* (Martínez, 2022), *Kitty Kakes* (Navarro and Rocha, 2022). *Wild Life Games* created the card games *Wild Life: The Card Game* (Alamo Borja et al., 2021) (in collaboration with Axo Studios) and *Wild Life Mayan Be'et* (Dzib, 2022b). Dice Games like *Coffee Dice* (Martínez, 2019), *Piñata Dice* (Esparza, 2020), and party games such as *Party Booster* (Crosswind Games, 2019) and *Cooking Rumble* (Estrada Lucero, 2018). Please note that I'm explicitly leaving out Mexican Trading Card Games (TCG) and Role-Playing Games (RPG) as I consider them different media.

We can observe common trends here. The first one is that from 2017 onwards, there was a rapid increase in game development. Now, board game designers are always looking to create new mechanics and explore exciting and attractive settings. Due to the high demand for Eurogames worldwide, given the pandemic, Mexican game designers face much competition. This is a natural result: "The producer of technological forms – in this case, the game designer – is also plagued, but with … the problem of having to constantly innovate" (Murray, 2018, 17). The only way to reach consolidation is to publish new games continuously, but this wears out creativity and attention from the public. This leads us to another feature.

It is notorious that Mexican indie developers publish games with names in English, even if the ruleset is in Spanish (or in the two languages). Game designers in Mexico must struggle for visibility. One way to gain recognition is to appeal first to the public worldwide, a possibility available thanks to the use of the English language. Fortunately, there are conventions devoted exclusively to board games, such as the *Mega XP* in Mexico City and the *Roll a Game Expo* in Guadalajara, which are well-established and gaining prestige. Conventions are familiar places to promote board games and are essential for game designers. Meanwhile, players and game designers tend to gather at local shops.

Another common feature is the use of crowdfunding platforms. Mexican game designers have found *Kickstarter* particularly attractive, and now a large part of the gaming community visit the page daily to check for new games. However, crowdfunding is no guarantee of success. Such is the case of e.g. *Against the Gods,* which will be relaunched as *All-Fathers* in 2024, as has happened with many other titles.

The Problem of Unearthing the Mesoamerican Heritage

Once we have recognized the challenges of board designers, it is time we problematized the postcolonial features and contemporary gaming in Mexico, which constantly oscillates between catching up with Western trends, discernible in the proliferation of Eurogames, and invoking Mesoamerican themes to assert Mexican identity unambiguously. As said before, one of the pillars of *Criollo*'s identity was to appropriate the pre-Hispanic heritage to validate their position in the New World against the *Peninsulares*. Then, the *Mestizo* society inherited this behavior, blurring the barriers between drawing symbolic content from the pre-Hispanic cultures as true inheritors or doing so as a *Criollo* unconscious need of legitimacy. It is important to notice that very recently, a new category has emerged to describe people in Mexico that somehow take the place of the *Criollo*. They are called "Whitexicans" (Rejón, 2020). It is not clear where or when the neologism appeared. Still, it is used in Social Networks to point out to a privileged minority that is ignorant (either consciously or unconsciously) of the enormous inequalities and discrimination in the country, resulting from the preservation of dispossession from the postcolonial institutions, as it has happened in other places (Mukherjee, 2017).

"Whitexican" has become a pejorative term, and they are criticized for their colonizing behavior and cultural appropriation. Hence, there is an evident problem for Mexicans with board game design. Who is creating board games in Mexico, the *Criollos*, the *Mestizos* or the "Whitexicans"? When creating games, specifically Eurogames with Mesoamerican themes, Mexicans risk falling into a *Criollo* necessity and, in that way, a self-colonization.

Representation in board games is immensely important for diversity and inclusion (Booth, 2021, 177). That's why contemporary designers look for authenticity and tie their games to themes related to their cultural heritage. However, in the case of Mexican games themed around Mexican or pre-Hispanic heritage, I pose an uncomfortable question: who is being represented here? New board games seldom reach the indigenous people. Moreover, new games fail to reach a large part of the population who does not have an advantageous economic situation. Of course, these questions are not meant to stop game design. According to Murray, one of the directions of postcolonial game studies is to produce "an ongoing commitment to social awareness and self-reflexivity within the larger context of understanding one's self as part of a public sphere" (Murray, 2018, 20). In this way, it entails a "radical move away from comfort zones of the resolution and an embrace of the ongoing position of alterity" (Murray, 2018, 21). I agree with Murray's position on the connection between games and politics. Gamer communities tend to depoliticize gaming, but this is impossible. Colonization, representation, diversity, and inclusion are timely and political topics. "[T]he popular depoliticization of video games as part of a larger perception that they do not constitute a part of culture contributes to a troubling and persistent lack of complex engagement with this dimension of games" (Murray, 2018, 9). My work aims to open these questions to postcolonial game studies in Mexico. How can players and designers create games that get in touch with Mexican people and minorities? How can we create a sensual and baroque effect like what happens with the *Lotería*?

Mexican Board Games and Mesoamerican Heritage

A dozen games from the above list are explicitly related to Mexican themes. Early Eurogames like *La Tumba del Rey Pakal* focused on Mesoamerican heritage – in this case, Mayan. It is a strategic game devoted to exploring the Palenque archeological zone and was authorized by the Mexican National Institute of Anthropology and History (INAH). On the contrary, some games involve Mesoamerican motifs only as decoration, such as *Ts'Unu'Um* (hummingbird in Mayan), a card game about hummingbirds, and *Ollinkalli*. *Lords of Xibalba* uses themes from Mayan mythology. Instead, the games *Ofrendados*, *Pátzcuaro,* and *Terrorxico* are meant to celebrate Mexican heritage. *Ofrendados* is a strategic game revolving around the Nahuatl underworld, the Mictlan, and the *Día de Muertos* (Day of the Death). Also, *Pátzcuaro* includes a similar theme for its mechanics. *Terrorxico* is a semi-cooperative card game about hunting Mexican legends and mythological monsters. *Amapotoliztli Tonalpohualli is* card game (Rodríguez Mota and Sánchez Chávez n.d.) based on the Nahuatl calendar (*Tonalpohuall*). It consists of a deck of cards closer to traditional games and offers several variants, including a *Lotería* one. *Amapotoliztli Tonalpohualli* is a clear case that is meant to recover or reconnect with pre-Hispanic heritage by putting together specific cultural artifacts, cards, traditional games, and astrological pre-Hispanic themes. As it reads on their web page "The Count of the Days card game pays homage to the richness of our culture with a design based on the 5 x 9 ratio present in the stepped fretwork and its illustrations based on plate 1 of the Fejérváry Mayer codex" (Rodríguez Mota and Sánchez Chávez, n.d., translation mine).

Two recent games deserve a particular comment. *Moctezuma* (Escalante and Escalante, 2021a) is a Eurogame published by Devir. It preserves a Manichaean discourse of warfare and confrontation between cultures. Its summary reads "Moctezuma is a cooperative board game: the players work together to defeat the Spanish and defend Tenochtitlan. If we succeed, we all win, but if the Spanish win, we all lose. It is the first game to combine this style with a pre-Hispanic theme" (Escalante and Escalante, 2021a, translation mine).

Instead, if one would look for games exploring Mexican heritage without relation to conquest and dominance, one of the fresh and original takes is *Museo de la Cultura Mexica* (*The Museum of Mexica Culture*) (Juárez and Christiansen, 2022), a very recent game funded on *Kickstarter* early in 2022. It is written in both Spanish and English. It is a horror, semi-cooperative strategic game where players explore a copy of the National Museum of Anthropology and History in Mexico City. At the same time, they escape from one of the players acting as a "Ghost Priest" looking for sacrifices. The *Kickstarter* presentation summarizes the novel approach to Mexican heritage:

> The Museum of Mexica Culture is a place located in downtown Mexico City. It was built during the colonial era of the country, on top of the ruins of the Mexica civilization, which existed in these lands for centuries. This civilization was enslaved, massacred, and stolen from their territory to make way for the conquerors: the museum walls were build with the same rocks that formed ancient and sacred temples, stained with the blood of the indigenous civilization, which originally founded this city. Many vestiges of this civilization co-exist with the daily environment, and the accelerated pace of the City: The ruins of the Templo Mayor (a neighboring relic of our museum, which you can visit with the same access ticket!).
>
> (Juárez and Christiansen, 2022)

The game explicitly acknowledges the confluence of cultures, the baroque situation of being in a society built by conquerors and pre-Hispanic cultures, not hiding the atrocities underwent by the indigenous people of the Americas.

Conclusions

We have discussed the sources of Mexican identity and how traditional board games have contributed to creating a space for self-recognition in independent Mexico. Mexican culture is still ruled by *criollismo,* a synthetic consciousness of being both an heir of the Spanish conquerors and a proud possessor of the indigenous past of New Spain. Studying the particularities of Mexican identity, we try to answer some relevant questions for postcolonial game studies, such as "What are the presumptive qualities of those who play?" (Mukherjee, 2016). As we have seen, because of *criollismo,* the situation in the board gaming community is challenging for Mexican game developers. Designers need to stimulate the market, gain creative freedom, and popularize gaming, but as there are few ways available, the easiest is to appeal to the foreign public. At the same time, they must face the problem of games dealing with pre-Hispanic themes, which are attractive to *criollismo,* and simultaneously not involving themselves in perpetuating colonizing discourses. How can a game designer tackle these dilemmas? I have no definite answer, as it is not the intention of the chapter. However, I believe it lies on the grounds of Mexicanity, i.e., in the dichotomy of falling and not falling into the abyss of *barroco.*

As Mochocki discusses, "Heritage is not history" (Mochocki, 2021, 8). Heritage is about redefining our relationship with our past to construct our present and imagine the future. *Lotería* is part of Mexican heritage because it matters to us; we identify with it and the story that it tells us. From the quantitative approach of modernity, which privileges functionality and machinery, Mexicans are barbaric, uncivilized, savage people, sunk up to our necks in backwardness, magic, ignorance, and superstition. According to that view, we live under useless categories that do not exalt symmetry. Nevertheless, *barroco* is not detrimental to Mexican heritage and culture; we just must understand and re-appropriate it. It has been a way of living and a result of the need to create a new identity. Yet, it is a way of living outside the Western trend, an alternative form of rationality to strive for otherness, one which affirms life, infinity, and possibilities.

I believe it is possible to look for a way of being in the world as Mexicans in the magical, mythological, surreal world of the *barroco.* Instead of adopting foreign thinking that is substantial, finished, mechanical, and perfect, if we search our roots and accept the *Criollo* identity critically, we might find a way to live according to our temperament and historical moment. Where the accident and contradictions of the Mexican make it possible to create, give color to the world and shape a concrete vitality that accepts, embraces, laughs, and mocks death itself. Mexico has its own historical way of integrating alterity, away from the standard European (and enlightened). It is vital to explore how Mexican board games, as cultural artifacts, could exploit this advantage to help strive for a postcolonial perspective of the world. It does not matter if they are Eurogames or just Mexican games.

Recognizing heritage is essential for the symbolic transformation and renegotiation of our position concerning the rationalistic and utilitarian Western thought. This work constitutes a preliminary approach that draws content from philosophy and the history of ideas and needs to relate to the actual people who play board games in Mexico. A complete demographic analysis of players and designers is necessary as an ethnographic study that addresses the problems of representation, diversity, and inclusion. Moreover, it would be interesting to compare the Mexican case with other Latin-American countries that underwent a similar colonial process. I hope this work sparks the discussion toward reflective play and what is to play and design board games in Mexico and Latin America.

References – books

Aspe Armella, V., *Las aporías fundamentales del periodo novohispano*. Mexico City: CONACULTA, 2002. [In Spanish]

Berlin, Isaiah, *The Roots of Romanticism*. Princeton, NJ: Princeton University Press, 2013.

Booth, Paul, *Board Games as Media*. New York, NY: Bloomsbury Academic, 2021.

Bustillo, C., *Barroco y América Latina. Un itinerario inconcluso*. Caracas: Monte Ávila Editores, 1988. [In Spanish]

de la Cruz, Sor Juana Inés, *Primero sueño y otros escritos*. México: Fondo de Cultura Económica, 2006. [In Spanish]

Deleuze, G., *The Fold: Leibniz and the Baroque*. Minneapolis, MN: Minnesota University Press, 1992.

Enriquez Vázquez, Armando, January 11, 2021. "La historia de Montecarlo, la marca mexicana de juegos de mesa sin ser un casino." *The Point. La revista online de marketing.* http://thepoint.com.mx/2021/01/11/la-historia-de-montecarlo-la-marca-mexicana-de-juegos-de-mesa-sin-ser-un-casino/ [In Spanish]

García Saiz, Maria Concepción, *Las castas mexicanas. Un genero pictorico americano*. No place identified: Olivetti, 1989.

González y González, Luis, et al., *Juegos y Juguetes Mexicanos*. México: Dina, Fundación Cultural CREMI, 1993. [In Spanish]

López Farjeat, L. J. and Zagal Arreguín, H., *Dos aproximaciones estéticas a la identidad nacional*. Nuevo León: Universidad Autónoma de Nuevo León, 1998. [In Spanish]

Masera Ceruti, Marian (Ed). *Colección Chávez Cedeño: Antonio Vanegas Arroyo: Un editor extraordinario*. Ciudad de México: Universidad Nacional Autónoma de México, 2017. [In Spanish]

Mochocki, Michal, *Role-play as a Heritage Practice Historical Larp, Tabletop RPG and Reenactment*. London: Routledge, 2021.

Mukherjee, Souvik, *Videogames and Postcolonialism. Empire Plays Back*. London: Palgrave McMillan, 2017.

Mukherjee, Souvik, 2016. "Playing Subaltern: Video Games and Postcolonialism." *Games and Culture*, 13 (5), pp. 504–520.
Mukherjee, S. and Hammar, E., 2018. "Introduction to the Special Issue on Postcolonial Perspectives in Game Studies." *Open Library of Humanities*. 4: pp. 33.
Murray, Soraya, 2018. "The Work of Postcolonial Game Studies in the Play of Culture." *Open Library of Humanities*, 4 (1): 13, pp. 1–25.
O'Gorman, E., *Meditaciones sobre el criollismo*. Mexico City: Centro de Historia de México Condumex. México, 1970. [In Spanish]
Ortiz Lanz, José Enrique, ¡*Lotería!: un mundo de imágenes: las loterías de figuras en Campeche y México*. México: Cámara de Diputados (México). LXIII Legislatura. Consejo Editorial, 2017.
Ramos, Samuel, *El perfil del hombre y la cultura en México*. Madrid: Austral, 1951.
Rejón, René, September 24, 2020. "Whitexican: una definición balanceada." *Animal Político*. https://www.animalpolitico.com/blog-invitado/whitexican-una-definicion-balanceada/ [In Spanish]
Schlarman, Joseph H. L., *Mexico, a Land of Volcanoes, from Cortes to Aleman*. Milwaukee, WI: Bruce Publishing Company, 1950.
de Sepúlveda, Juan Ginés. *Apología: De Juan Gines de Sepúlveda contra Fray Bartolomé de las Casas y de Fray Bartolomé de las Casas contra Juan Gines de Sepúlveda*. Madrid: Ed. Nacional, 1975.
Uranga, E., *Análisis del ser del mexicano y otros escritos sobre la filosofía de la mexicano*. México City: Bonilla Artigas Editores, 2013. [In Spanish]
Woods, Stewart, *Eurogames: The Design, Culture and Play of Modern European Board Games*. Jefferson, NC: McFarlan & Company, 2009.
Zapata Flores, C., *El juego y sus raíces. Un acercamiento simbólico a la identidad cultural de un pueblo*. 2010. [In Spanish]

References – games

Alamo Borja, Adrian, Camacho, Mich, and Cordoba, Leo, *Wild Life: The Card Game* [Card game]. Mexico: Axo Stories, Wild Life Games, 2021. https://boardgamegeek.com/boardgame/304666/wild-life-card-game
Alamo Borja, Adrian, Macba, Pepe, and Valdés, Victor, *Party Panda Pirates* [Board game]. Mexico: Detestable Games, Draco Studios, 2022. https://boardgamegeek.com/boardgame/365119/party-panda-pirates
Armijo Castro, Armando, *False God's Fall* [Board game]. México: Self-published, 2020. https://fgf.mx/
Arroyo, Juan, *Ollinkalli* [Board game]. Mexico: Arroyo Ibarra & Asociados, 2016. https://arqarroyo.wixsite.com/inicio?pgid=jg5qchrq-0c70439b-6133-4fa9-83f4-8d907a69ff56
Artigas, Santos and Jager, Kina, *Meeplepalooza* [Board game]. Mexico: Detestable Games, 2018. https://boardgamegeek.com/boardgame/255395/meeplepalooza
Ayala, Andrés, *Seat Wars* [Board game]. Mexico: Detestable Games, Aether Tower, 2018. https://boardgamegeek.com/boardgame/239907/seat-wars
Bayardo Dodge, Maria Lucia, *Yortuk* [Board game]. Mexico: Editorial Morenike, 2016. https://boardgamegeek.com/boardgame/357946/yortuk
Benitez López, Omar Isai, *Fotozoo* [Board game]. Mexico: Ludens Games, 2021. https://boardgamegeek.com/boardgame/330369/fotozoo

Burgos, William and Ramos, Juan, *Tricksters* [Board game]. Mexico: Aether Tower, 2016. https://boardgamegeek.com/boardgame/205604/tricksters

Cabrera Fernández, Juan José, *Chakkan: The Card Game* [Board game]. Mexico: Another B Game, 2019.

Calderón Espinoza, José Adán, *Rolling Farmers* [Board game]. Mexico: Ludens Games, 2021. https://tabletopia.com/games/rolling-farmers

Coronado, Ana, *Geisha* [Board game]. Mexico: Detestable Games, 2019. https://boardgamegeek.com/boardgame/253434/geisha

Cortés, Luis Alfredo, *Adigma* [Board game]. Mexico: Ludika y Artefactos, 2012a. https://adigma.com.mx/adigma/

Cortés, Luis Alfredo, *Adidoku* [Board game]. Mexico: Ludika y Artefactos, 2012b. https://adigma.com.mx/adidoku/

Cortés, Luis Alfredo, *Rana Sapiens* [Board game]. Mexico: Lúdica y Artefactos, 2022. https://adigma.com.mx/ranasapiens/

Corza, Adrián and Uribe, Roberto, *Microcosmos* [Board game]. Mexico: BorreCorp, 2019.

Donovan, Alegria, et al., *Make a Boys Love Story* [Board game]. México: Estudio 26.5, 2022. https://www.kickstarter.com/projects/nacazona/make-a-boys-love-story

Dzib, Ricardo, *Aban!* [Board game]. México: Lighthouse Games, 2022a. https://www.lighthousegms.com/aban

Dzib, Ricardo, *Wild Life Mayan Be'et* [Board game]. Mexico: Wild Life Games, 2022b. https://boardgamegeek.com/boardgame/364861/wild-life-mayan-beet

Escalante, Iván, *Necronomicorp* [Board game]. México: Mulligan Creative, 2016. https://www.gnomosapiens.com/necronomicorp

Escalante, Iván, *Card Game: The Card Game* [Board game]. México: Gnomosapiens, 2019. https://www.gnomosapiens.com/cardgamethecardgame

Escalante, Iván, *Backyard of Frutabaja* [Board game]. México: Gnomosapiens, 2021a. https://www.gnomosapiens.com/boardgames

Escalante, Iván, *Filler Clash* [Board game]. México: Mulligan Creative, 2021b. https://www.gnomosapiens.com/fillerclash

Escalante, Rafael and Escalante, Joel, *Cazadores de Fósiles*. México: Xiba Games, 2011a. https://xibagames.com/2020/10/cazadores-fosiles/

Escalante, Rafael and Escalante, Joel, *Tumba del Rey Pakal*. México: Xiba Games, 2011b. https://xibagames.com/2020/10/la-tumba-del-rey-pakal/

Escalante, Rafael and Escalante, Joel, *Jardín Botánico de Tehuacán*. México: Xiba Games, 2013. https://xibagames.com/2020/10/jardin-botanico/

Escalante, Joel and Escalante, Rafael, *Moctezuma*. México: Devir, 2021a. https://devir.mx/producto/moctezuma/

Escalante, Joel and Escalante Rafael, *Turtle Splash* [Board game]. Mexico: Gigamic, 2021b. https://boardgamegeek.com/boardgame/343833/turtle-splash

Escalante Hernández, Gener, *TerrorXico* [Board game]. Mexico: Self-published, 2018. https://boardgamegeek.com/boardgame/228370/terrorixico

Esparza, Carlos, *Piñata Dice* [Board game]. Mexico: Esparza Games, 2020. https://boardgamegeek.com/boardgame/332871/pinata-dice

Esteva, Alejandro, *Lords of Xibalba* [Board game]. México: Detestable Games, 2018. https://boardgamegeek.com/boardgame/251450/lords-xibalba

Estrada Lucero, Emilio Gerardo, *Cooking Rumble* [Board game]. México: Aether Tower, 2018. https://boardgamegeek.com/boardgame/227163/cooking-rumble

Fernandez, Victor, *Toongeon Fights* [Board game]. Mexico: Arlon Games, 2022. https:// boardgamegeek.com/boardgame/359809/toongeon-fights

Guizar, José, *Infected: The Board Game* [Board game]. México: GZRI Games, 2017. https://boardgamegeek.com/boardgame/217488/infected-board-game

Gutman Duering, Federico, *Cook King* [Board game]. México: Bravou Games, 2022.

Hernández, Rubén, *Dragons of the Red Moon: The Gauntlet* [Board game]. México: Draco Studios, 2019a.

Hernández, Rubén, *Pátzcuaro* [Board game]. Mexico: Detestable Games, 2019b. https://boardgamegeek.com/boardgame/267010/patzcuaro

Hernández, Ronald, *Las Mañas del Poder [Board game]*. Mexico: Self-published, 2022. https://quepario.com/products/las-manas-del-poder-preventa-de-la-segunda-edicion

Hernández, Rubén and Escalante, Iván, *Dodos Riding Dinos* [Board game]. México: Draco Studios and Detestable Games, 2021. https://www.dracostudios.com/ dodos-riding-dinos

Juárez, A. I. and Christiansen, L., *Museo de la Cultura Mexica*. México: Self-published, 2022. https://www.kickstarter.com/projects/aldoiram/museo-de-la-cultura-mexica?lang=es Lighthouse Games https://www.lighthousegms.com/es/ games

López Valdepeña, Ramón, *Kanyimajo:* [Board Game]. México: Guerra Gato Games, 2016a. https://boardgamegeek.com/boardgame/278226/kanyimajo

López Valdepeña, Ramón, *Guerras Gato:* [Board Game]. México: Guerra Gato Games, 2016b. https://boardgamegeek.com/boardgame/219574/guerras-gato

López Valdepeña, Ramón, *Bakenero: Soul Reaper* [Board Game]. México: Guerra Gato Games, 2018. https://boardgamegeek.com/boardgame/264732/bakeneko-soul-reaper

Luna, Lis, *Dark Maiden* [Board game]. México: Sunfairy games, 2018. https://boardgamegeek.com/boardgame/298487/dark-maiden

Luna Lis, *Party Warriors* [Board game]. Mexico: Detestable Games, 2019. https:// boardgamegeek.com/boardgame/285655/party-warriors

Luzarreta, Adrián. *Hitodama* [Board game]. Mexico: Lighthouse Games, 2012. https:// www.lighthousegms.com/hitodama

Luzarreta, Adrián. *Doxa: The Card Game* [Board game]. Mexico: Lighthouse Games, 2018. https://www.lighthousegms.com/es/doxa

Macba, Pepe and Escalante, Iván, *Kiwi Chow Down* [Board game]. Mexico: Detestable Games, Draco Studios and Board Zeppelin, 2022. https://www.kickstarter.com/ projects/detestablegames/kiwi-chow-down?ref=dracowebsite

Martínez, Quetzalcóatl, *Coffee Dice* [Board game]. México: Self-published, 2019. https://boardgamegeek.com/boardgame/279082/coffee-dice

Martínez, Alexz, *Kaikoro* [Board game]. México: Rawr Games, 2022.

Mendez, Iván, *Chronicles of Marlis* [Board game]. México: Kursed Games, Self-published, 2021.

Moya, Sofía, *Souvenirs* [Board game]. Mexico: Ludens Games, 2021. https://boardgamegeek.com/boardgame/320102/souvenirs

Muñoz, Luis and Novelo, Andrés. *Cooks & Crooks* [Board game]. México: Detestable Games, 2019.

Navarro, Lviz and Rocha, Yamile, *Kitty Kakes* [Board game]. México: Lvzoria Games Lab, 2022.

Party Booster [Board game]. Mexico: Crosswind Games, 2019. https://www.party-booster.mx/

Perez Tovar, Carlos David, *Weapon Wars* [Board game]. Mexico: Lodus Games, 2019. https://boardgamegeek.com/boardgame/257316/weapon-wars

Perez Tovar, Carlos David, *Ofrendados* [Board game]. Mexico: Puercomonte, 2021. https://puercomonte.com/?page_id=4050&v=267d696eab9e

Ramos, Israel, *Folclore* [Board game]. Mexico: Ludens Games, 2019a. https://boardgamegeek.com/boardgame/304029/folclore

Ramos, Israel, *Colorbugs* [Board game]. Mexico: Ludens Games, 2019b. https://boardgamegeek.com/boardgame/304030/colorbugs

Ramos, Israel, *Pájaros en el Alambre* [Board game]. Mexico: Ludens Games, 2020. https://boardgamegeek.com/boardgame/334290/pajaros-en-el-alambre

Rodríguez Mota, Jorge César and Sánchez Chávez, Lucila Y., *Amapotoliztli Tonalpohualli* [Board game]. Mexico: Self-published, n.d. https://naipesat.webs.com/

Rolón, Rubén, *Against the Gods* [Board game]. Mexico: Moneta Games, 2022a. https://www.facebook.com/monetagames/

Rolón, Rubén, *Eris: Seed of Discord* [Board game]. Mexico: Moneta Games, 2022b. https://www.facebook.com/monetagames/

Sanchez, Saúl, *Tierra y Libertad: Mexican Revolution* [Board game]. Mexico: Malinche games, 2018. https://boardgamegeek.com/boardgame/242191/tierra-y-libertad-mexican-revolution-game-second-e

Sánchez, Salvador. *Antes del diluvio* [Board game]. Mexico: Ludens Games, 2019. https://boardgamegeek.com/boardgame/334291/antes-del-diluvio

Sanchez, Saúl, *Timeline Revolution* [Board game]. Mexico: Malinche games, 2020. https://www.malinchegames.com/en_us/timeline-revolution/

Sanchez, Saul, *Patria Libre* [Board game]. Mexico: Malinche Games, 2022. https://tabletopia.com/games/patria-libre-the-struggle-for-mexican-independence

Suarez Olivares, Miguel, *Bite and Treaty*. [Board game]. Mexico: Lighthouse Games, 2022. https://www.lighthousegms.com/biteandtreaty

Suarez Olivares, Miguel and Giordano, Grianfranco, *Neuroriders* [Board game]. Mexico: Maso Games, 2022. https://boardgamegeek.com/boardgame/350992/neuroriders

Whiu, Gerardo, *Tattoo Brawl* [Board game]. Mexico: Self-published, 2019. https://boardgamegeek.com/boardgame/282390/tattoo-brawl

Zamora, Adrián, *Ts'Unu'Um* [Board game]. Mexico: Moneta Games, 2022.

6 The Brazilian (Gamer) Culture through the Lenses of Nostalgia

An Analysis of *Brazil: Imperial*

Thiago Pereira Falcão

Alexander Carneiro

Introduction

Games do not exist apart from society, culture, and "day-to-day" life, for culture and ideology flow into game design and playing practices. When games depict the historical past as a glorious and less problematic time, they use nostalgia, contributing to reinterpreting history and collective memory. This process can help support the emergence and maintenance of radical ideologies, sterilizing the past of its ties with the systemic violence of colonization, downplaying or even completely suppressing it, while naturalizing symbolic and physical violence.[1]

Brazil: Imperial is a peculiar object: it helps produce nostalgia, itself being a product of it. It manifests images and discourses that depict the Brazilian Empire Era as glorious, abundant with heroes and social advancements, thus providing an opportunity to explore how the media usually depicts the historical period and what the relationship between games and history conveys about the country's cultural heritage, memory, and identity. The game was successful in Brazil, which prompted many reviews and mostly positive comments from the community (Covil dos Jogos, 2020; Tábula Quadrada, 2022), though it had its share of discontent from players dissatisfied with how the game represented its central themes.[2,3] Our exploration of the game follows Paul Booth's ludo-textual analysis (2021), reading the board game as a text, and combining game texts and mechanical structures to understand how the game conveys meaning.

Brazil: Imperial happens at an interesting cultural crossroads: the recent tendency toward political conservativeness dubbed "a Brazilian far-right neoliberal nationalism" (Iamamoto et al., 2021), which has been mobilizing many adepts of video gaming and the gaming culture to its ranks (Falcão et al., 2020a, 2020b, 2021). Such context helps foster a welcoming environment to the imagined colonial and imperial past, overlooking gaps regarding

DOI: 10.4324/9781003356318-6

historical violence toward cultural and ethnic groups that do not conform to white masculinity. This chapter builds up from this cultural context to explore how board games can help advance a conservative agenda through the use of nostalgia.

Nostalgia for the Brazilian History

One of the most notorious political facts in Brazil's recent history is the 1993 referendum, which consulted the population about the political system. Though the republican presidential system won, parliamentary republic and monarchy were also included as options. This fact illustrates a phenomenon that Brazilian historian Ricardo Salles (2013) calls Imperial Nostalgia: a feeling of nostalgia for the monarchical regime under which Brazil lived between 1822 when it declared its independence from Portugal, and 1889 when it suffered its first military coup, with the Proclamation of the Republic.

The gamer culture recurrently seeks to establish a relationship with the past, fostering a nostalgic desire that reimagines history in an uncomplicated mode (Salter and Blodgett, 2017). This phenomenon is related to how games establish a dialogue with the Medieval Era and its tropes (Young, 2016): it "is related to the emotions that connect us to the use of our modern reception of the Middle Ages" (Fedriga, 2021) – or, in a more stylistic form, "America, having come to grips with 1776, is devouring the Real Past" (Eco 1986, 62). Nostalgia reasserts itself as an influential cultural and emotional force that constitutes the past as an inaccessible ideal in comparison to the reality of the present (Coontz, 2000).

This understanding of nostalgia not as a feeling (Boym 2001, 37) but as a way to reimagine and relive the past is key to the objective of this work. From this perspective, Boym (2001) discusses how contemporary society uses, for example, the presence of dinosaurs in the media: "dinosaurs are ideal animals for the nostalgia industry because nobody remembers them. Their extinction guarantees commercial success; it allows for total restoration and global exportability." Boym's (2001) argument addresses the performance of remembering, the production of memory as a dramatic, rather than factual, reconstitution of the past.

In the case of the Latin American experience, Walter Mignolo (1991) discusses how modernity and capitalism (including its neoliberal form) have contributed to the suppression of indigenous knowledge and cultural practices. The implementation of the neoliberal system and the promotion of free trade and globalization has led to the displacement of indigenous communities and the loss of traditional cultural practices, which adds up to the emergence of a "coloniality" – an effect in which the cultural and economic practices of the global North have been imposed on the Global South.

The spread of neoliberalism is accompanied by the "globalization of Western episteme," in which the West's dominant cultural and intellectual traditions have been imposed on the rest of the world (Mignolo, 1991). In addition, by "typically celebrating ephemerality and short-term contracts" (Harvey, 2005), neo-liberalization contributes to the erasure of collective memory and cultural identities, reinforcing the conflict between history and the present. This encourages the deterioration of the past to an instrumentalization of its carefully selected parts. What seems like a digression here helps to approach the typical attitude in-game design: appropriating elements of the past, sterilizing them from aberrant colonial violence, and flattening them into innocent and uncritical amusement (Pullen, 2018; Muñoz, 2022).

The history of the Brazilian Empire is significantly different from that of colonial Brazil. Rampant exploitation and crimes against native peoples under a civilizing rhetoric mark the colonial period. The imperial period, in turn, is marked "by the greatness of the nation and its rulers, mainly D. Pedro II, and by administrative probity" (Salles, 2013, loc. 56). This view is often re-enacted in contemporary times: either in the perception of the city of Rio de Janeiro as the most culturally important for the country, despite its social deterioration (see Arantes and Rezende, 2023); but also in the way various national media approach the period, commonly representing it as the Brazilian Belle Époque. Dom Pedro II, who assumed the throne of the Empire in 1831, is often depicted as kind, Christian, and progressive – committed to human rights such as education and health.[4]

However, the period's social history is considerably different from its depiction in today's media. Salles (2013) underlines that even though Brazilian culture continues to work from a nostalgic representation that glorifies this idyllic past, one cannot separate slavery from imperial politics. "The institutional edifice of the Second Reign was solid because it rested on the material strength and wealth generated by slavery" (loc. 70). The Crown, the party of the seigniorial class, performed a civilizing mission in the configuration of the imperial nation (Salles, 2013), seeking to imbue it with a European root that sought to preserve and restore the large export property of colonial origin: slavery. This civilizing process, maintaining the slaveholding order, was responsible for implanting these ideals into the republic, making them pillars of the Brazilian republican society. This process was far from accidental; it is essential to perceive it as a project. The establishment of the Empire as this idyllic place represented, for historians, politicians, and intellectuals, a moral reserve that reinforced the exclusionary republican order. Salles (2013) emphasizes that this nostalgia was present in the 1920s, resonated strongly in the 1950s, and, finally, appeared refreshed in the 1990s due to political issues of the day – namely, the disappointment of Brazilian society with the republican status quo due to the numerous cases of corruption that plagued the media narrative at that moment.

The concept of nostalgia is critical for interpreting *Brazil: Imperial*, as it helps contextualize its production in the context of the political instability Brazil has been going through since the mid-early 2010s. Although our goal is to build an argument about Imperial Nostalgia – a sentiment foundational to the formation of Brazilian society (Salles, 2013) – it is impossible to detach the game's conception and production, as well as its authorial dimension,[5] from the recent rise of conservatism: a surge that strongly alludes to a nostalgic militaristic feeling that yearns for the various dictatorships in recent Brazilian history. Consider that this is a game produced under the aegis of the government of Jair Bolsonaro, a former president avowedly aligned with the ideals of the Far-Right, who continually addresses himself as "sent from God,"[6] "the defender of the country against communism"[7] or the great knight of Christian morality.

Brazilian Gamer Culture

The emergence of gamer culture in Brazil closely intertwines with the local history of technology and, more centrally, with the stratification of social classes. Video games were particularly relevant in the consumption scenario of children and teenagers with economically developed backgrounds during the 1980s and 1990s. From the 2000s on, they became a legitimate entertainment alternative, especially after the spread of video game rental stores – which decentralized consumption – and the cheapening of computers and accessories. These conditions were defining factors in articulating practices around this medium. Understanding gamer cultures in Brazil depends on comprehending the medium, its codes of use and consumption, and its material, political, and social context. These symbols, codes, and contexts are determinants of social practices and material conditions.

Brazil's video game and board game cultures coexist within the same social, historical, and cultural context. Such context is defining: game culture in Brazil is commonly associated with toxic behaviors related to performances of racism, exaggerated masculinity, and political extremism, typically stemming from conservative and nostalgic social postures. These iterations have been documented by researchers in the field of game studies, many of whom focus on how political and cultural conditions relate to online platforms – not only social media but also platforms that host gaming experiences, like Fortnite (Epic Games, 2017), Free Fire (Garena, 2017), Roblox (Roblox Corporation, 2006), among others. However, a schism between a digital and in-person social experience needs addressing in this perception. Falcão et al. (2021), for example, demonstrated that the performance in face-to-face gaming spaces – local game stores focused on competitive games – is often guided by conservative and nostalgic values, as well as in digital spaces.

Game scholars have discussed the ties between video games and colonization. Penix-Tadsen's book *Cultural Code* (2019), for example, criticizes that analyses of new media and culture reveal a critical tunnel vision. Penix-Tadsen's argument reiterates the vital fact that Latin America is the product of this process to the extent that many games that depict it cannot (or will not) dodge the theme. Board game scholars have also voiced their concerns about how colonialist tropes are approached. Borit et al. (2018) examine how three EUROGAMEs represented otherness from the colonizers' view, analyzing how the games depicted indigenous peoples' agency (or lack thereof) and culture. Foasberg (2016) discusses how Eurogames, despite not depicting violence, often choose to represent violent chapters in history, abstracting the indigenous other in this process. Beatriz Zapata adequately suggests that "one of the reasons for the success of [strategy] board games […] is that they always put the players in the shoes of the colonizers" (2020, 2), following it up with support for Souvik Mukherjee's question about the audience for these games and the very different gaming experiences for those who belong to former colonies or former colonial powers (2018).

The concern with a national gamer culture has only recently become relevant in Brazilian game studies. Discussions about appropriation and political literacy (Messias, 2016), conservatism and toxic masculinity (Falcão et al., 2021) or more focused on how neoliberalism as a cultural paradigm (Brown, 2019) dialogues with Brazilian gamer culture (Marques et al., 2021; Falcão et al., 2020a, 2020b) have been concerned with interpreting these practices through theoretical lenses committed to the relationships established between the gamer culture and the socio-historical contexts in Brazil. Some of those performances are dedicated explicitly to a conservative and nostalgic vision of history. Our question turns to how *Brazil: Imperial* promotes a positive reading of Brazil in its imperial period.

Observing the relationship between memory and the Brazilian gamer culture and how nostalgia is a mediating factor between the two is not a trivial exercise. Much of the prior criticism has sought to understand the immediate conditions of these cultural processes without necessarily holding onto the genealogical conditions – foldings, for Bruno Latour (2002) – of the production of these subjectivities. Thus, questioning the toxicity of Brazilian gamer culture (Kurtz, 2019) or the ability to adapt and overcome social inequality inherent to the Global South (Messias, 2016) without paying attention to its material and ontological conditions is a mere exercise of discussing symptoms, not grasping the problem in its radical form. It is necessary to depart from a historical standpoint to understand not only the technical aspects of games but their cultural surroundings and what ways of thinking they convey in the codification (inscription) of their mechanics and simulations. This exercise is undertaken, e.g., by Trammell (2021) in his discussion of learning aides used in children's literacy in the United States in the nineteenth century.

This line of thinking takes us along two separate paths: the first one studies the phenomenon narrated above by analyzing a material element – a board game. The second studies how the discourse in this board game is steeped in nostalgia and seeks to recreate bases for understanding and staging a past that comfortably ignores the hardships of the colonization process, committing to "a certain nostalgia for the time of the Empire that seems to linger in the Brazilian historical imaginary" (Salles, 2013, loc. 64). Let us read from Zapata (2020, 1) that living in a postcolonial era does not mean colonialism is in the past, but that there are "many neocolonial forms for maintaining Empire: racism, prejudice, lack of representation, the rise of the physical and psychological frontiers, exploitation, or global inequality, among many other."

Brazilian Board Games Culture

High prices mark the context of board game consumption in Brazil, with few companies, and an enthusiastic niche of hobbyist consumers, who find pleasure in playing and collecting different game titles. Board games have become popular mainly since the 2010s, accompanying the founding of one of the largest board game companies: Galápagos Jogos (Tolotti, 2022). In Brazil, there is also a substantial distinction between "classic" or "traditional board games" – and "modern board games" preferred by hobbyists.

In the board games community, the term "modern board game" addresses contemporary games created with certain design assumptions – inherited mainly from Eurogames. For Woods (2012, 16–17), so-called modern board games – or "hobby games" – differ from traditional board games because they are manufactured commodities produced for a specific niche market. This type of game can stimulate cultural formations around its elements, "which reflect both the moment in which they are produced and the identity and recreational choices of the players" (Woods, 2012, 17). In Brazil, hobbyist gamers refer to their favored types of games in the English language, "board game" and the ones they are less interested in as "Jogo de tabuleiro," the Portuguese equivalent term. This helps avoid confusion and provides easy identification. It also creates a hard line between games respected in the hobby and those not.

Brazil: Imperial was designed and published in Brazil, then translated and distributed abroad. It was a public and critical success that prompted many reviews (Covil dos Jogos, 2020; Tábula Quadrada, 2022), "let's play" videos, and forum entries. Costing currently more than a third of Brazil's minimum wage, the game boasts high-quality printed materials, painted wooden tokens, and more than 300 components in total, all of which are praised in reviews and comments. Reviewers cherished the fact that a Brazilian game displayed such a level of quality.

Though most reviewers and players complimented the game's theme, mechanics, and art, a few people voiced their concerns over how it depicted the Empire Era. In the Brazilian online board games forum Ludopedia, one post-titled "Problems with the theme" (April 18, 2021) shares concerns that the game might "disrespectfully represent indigenous and black people." Despite some comments on the post-agreeing with this assessment, most others dismiss these concerns as irrelevant and "too politically correct." Some additional comments reiterate the fact that "it is just a game" – implying that it should not be taken seriously – and that "good things happened during the Imperial period," which reinforces the already discussed way in which nostalgia for this period is still around.[8]

Colonialism, Eurogames, and *Brazil: Imperial*

Brazil: Imperial was designed by Zé Mendes and published in 2021 by MeepleBR. It can be played by up to 4 players, including a solo mode (MeepleBR, n.d.). It describes itself as a "Euro X," a "perfect mix" between Eurogames and the 4X genre (Ludopedia, n.d.). Each player controls a historical figure from the Brazilian Empire, such as Dom Pedro II, Isabella of Castile, and even Napoleon. Each player has an individual board, a different set of special abilities, and units that can be deployed onto the main board. Players compete over land to gather resources, expand and develop their empires to earn victory points, and win the game.

The board represents a map of a region in South America. It has a hexagonal grid divided into several irregular modules, which can be reassembled to represent different regions, each different in size and number of players. During setup, certain hexes on the map are covered by "exploration tiles." Players can "discover" these tiles when exploring the map by flipping them up and revealing them. These tiles can represent, among other things, unknown fauna to be collected or quilombo[9] communities, which are removed from the game after being explored and used for their respective bonuses. Exploring the map without facing any opposition, players traverse the game land with the sole purpose of exploring, exploiting, and conquering it. There is little attrition and almost no harmful consequences from exploring this unknown and (would-be) inhabited land. The game also almost lacks any indication of historical resistance against the Brazilian Empire – which alludes to the Eurogame tradition of avoiding representations of conflicts.

The only sign of resistance is when players discover an undefined red flag tile – defined only as "Expedition" – which they must defeat in exchange for victory points. The only different kind of conflict present in the game is between players themselves. Even the few nonwhite playable characters (Tibiriçá from the Tupiniquim people and Dom Obá II) are historically known for being friendly to the Portuguese colonizers or the

Brazilian Empire. The playable empires depicted in the game are impervious to rebellions and political struggle. The indigenous peoples are not enough to pose a threat or even to be represented on the map as holding any legitimate territory. In *Brazil: Imperial*, the only possible threats to establishing the player's empire are the external menaces posed by the other players – other Empires.

Players actively exploit and develop the explored land by extracting natural resources and building construction tiles on the map, such as the Gold Foundry, Farm Fields, or the Church. The players can gather resources, including brazilwood, sugar cane, cotton, and coffee, typical commodities produced throughout Brazil's history. Gold and science are unique resources that can be used to buy units and certain building tiles. These in-game mechanics may half-accurately simulate the techniques involved in the historical process of colonization, but they ignore the social impacts of such techniques. For example, the laborers who were to work the fields in this scenario would most certainly have been enslaved people. By literally removing any sign of workers and their struggle (not represented at all), the game arguably approaches history from an institutional point of view instead of critically evaluating the mentioned processes and methods. This emphasis on techniques instead of on the social impact of colonization is seen throughout the game and in the Eurogames category in general, as we will discuss soon.

On their turn, players can perform one action and move one unit to an adjacent tile on the board. Actions include "Deploy: Put a military unit on the board"; "Painting: Acquire a special character painting" from the available collection. These paintings depict famous characters from the Empire Era in Brazil, and each grants a special bonus; "Build: Put a building tile onto the board." This grants resources and expands the borders of the player's empire; "Renovate: Produce resources on a chosen building"; "Manufacture: Upgrade an Action" and receive extra bonuses from choosing said Action; "Harbor: Take one resource from the supply"; and "Trade: Exchange resources". These actions, seen together, tell the story of the Brazilian Empire through an executive institutional perspective. Action such as Build, Renovate, Harbor, and Trade, are related to managing resources and developing the land for production. The most peculiar action, not directly related to resource management, is the Painting action, allowing players to bring historical characters to their side. A sampling of the characters available to be acquired reveals that most, if not all of them, were seen as supporters of the Empire in one way or another. By choosing to portray only supporters of the Empire, the game puts forth a fictional homogenous scenario where opposition to the Empire and varied political views were nonexistent. This synthetic "Pax Brasilis" contributes to a vision of the past as a period where things were in order, less divided by contemporary politics.

Games are played along three "Eras." Each Era is triggered by accomplishing goals defined by mission cards, which can give each player medium-term goals and direct strategies. The game ends when players reach the third Era and count their victory points. Victory points are earned through exploring new lands, deploying military units, expanding borders, building cities, palaces, farms, and mines, and producing gold, science, and other resources. Through the configuration of which activities provide victory points, the game informs the types of gameplay it views as appropriate and wishes its players to execute. Such gameplay, we can assume, is based on the known historical behavior of empires: expansive and assimilative. It is also based on Brazil's understanding of its imperial period as a time of administrative efficiency and societal development (Salles, 2013), as that is, in fact, what players do in the game: manage the production and use of resources in the most efficient way possible to enable the cultural and scientific development of their empire. This form of scoring, which determines winners based on constructed buildings, resources produced, and conquered land, is well known in strategy games, from *Civilization* (MicroProse, 1991) to *Settlers of Catan* (Kosmos, 1995), and it helps position *Brazil: Imperial* in this genre.

As the game's description states, *Brazil: Imperial* does include elements from the Eurogames' tradition and the 4X genre. Players who explore the map, extract resources, and defend their borders with military units perform typical actions seen in 4X games. However, when the game asks players to manage resources, plan their actions and develop an efficient engine for generating victory points, they engage in the form of gameplay associated with Eurogames. Four distinctive traits make a Eurogame: (1) an emphasis on the game mechanics (formal structure) over theme or narrative; (2) the preference for indirect conflict between players over direct conflict; (3) the diminished role of luck and randomness to accentuate strategic choices and (4) a higher production quality of pieces and components (Woods, 2012).

The genre of Eurogames has a long and close relationship with colonialist themes, uncritically reproducing historical excerpts that have long been understood as problematic. The strategy Eurogame from 2002, *Puerto Rico*, is a clear example. In *Puerto Rico*, players represent colonizers on the island of the same name, managing resources, farming plantations, and controlling buildings by placing discs over them. Though referred to as "colonists" by the game manual, these components would historically be more accurately described as enslaved people, since they would have been the primary workforce in this period (Borit et al., 2018). By not understanding the discs as real people represented in the game, *Puerto Rico* (Ravensburger, 2002) ends up reproducing a pattern of behavior associated with enslaved people: working ceaselessly, being treated as resources, and without any subjectivity. *Brazil: Imperial* goes further on this erasure and completely removes workers from the game, transforming the production of resources into an abstract process that manifests after the command of the empire's ruler. There is no mention of enslaved people, slavery, or the abolition of slavery throughout the whole game and rulebook. Though it can be understood that the developers would not want to approach such a theme in the game, it is clear that, thematically and historically, the players' actions in-game would be directly benefiting from the effects of slavery. By not mentioning this critical chapter in Brazilian history, the game continues to effectively dodge any possible critiques of the Empire Era, contributing to the current imaginary regarding the time as unproblematic.

Conclusions

The construction of the nostalgic past in *Brazil: Imperial* takes two concurrent paths. First, it diminishes colonization's most brutal social impacts by transforming them into a matter of mechanics for resource production. In this way, the most questionable processes systematically undertaken by the Brazilian Empire – namely, the slavery politics and the extermination of indigenous people – are abstracted, and the focus diverges to material and social technologies: sawmills and farms, cities and canons. This uncritical portrayal effectively exempts the Brazilian Empire from some of its worst connotations, which helps create a positive image. There are no unethical decisions in *Brazil: Imperial*. There are also no ethical decisions. The game design choices lift the dimension of morality from the reality of the game.

The second path in which the game builds this nostalgic past is glorification of its apparently most positive aspects, featured as prime characteristics of the game. This can be seen in the playable characters, called monarchs, and the portrait paintings, highlighting those personalities that could only be understood as heroes of that period. These ideals of nobility bring the Brazilian historical past closer to the imagined Medieval Europe, which grants it an extra layer of legitimacy. Another example of emphasizing what is seen as good is the depiction of the territory now known as Brazil as a vast and uninhabited map, ready to be discovered and conquered, and abundant in natural riches to be exploited. The game also presents fauna and flora as bonuses to be found and used, depicting the land as full of natural resources. This approach mimics the first colonizers' view of the Americas, which highlighted the possibilities for the exploitation of natural resources.

Anachronisms further the notion that *Brazil: Imperial*'s vision of the country's past is based on a reimagined history. The emphasis on the bountiful nature of the land and on the vastness of the unknown territory resembles the sixteenth-century Colonial Brazil: an interpretation reinforced by the presence of the cotton and sugarcane resources. This contrasts with the monarchs, the painting cards, the text, and the coffee resource, more closely associated with the nineteenth-century Empire. This jumbling up of historical references creates an anachronistic patchwork of Brazil's past, one that can display its pleasant traits while obscuring its most vile realities.

Finally, it is worth returning to the construction of nostalgia. We can notice that the representation of the Empire in this game follows much of the same fascination that Eco (1986) sees in the American perception of the Middle Ages. What we seek to imply is that the connection we Brazilians have, as a nation, with the imperial period is similar to the one the West has with the Middle Ages. The commitment to the Empire of Brazil is a return to a time when it seemed we were building a free, egalitarian and fraternal society – as long as we carefully ignored the pillars supporting this structure. To think of the Empire as this ideal place is a way that Brazilian culture finds to relate to a past that is often sold as glorious. In this sense, thinking about this relationship between nostalgia and Brazilian history reaffirms the fact that even when we try to instrumentalize an understanding of our history, this process is done through the lens of Mignolo's coloniality: the desire to belong to a glorious past often overrides our history – unimportant, and buried under the debris left by the rise of neoliberalism.

Notes

1 Achille Mbembe. 2019. offers a comprehensive account of the deeds and heritages of colonization in "Necropolitics" (2016).
2 Ludopedia. 2021. "Problemas na Temática?" Fórum. Accessed December 21, 2022. https://ludopedia.com.br/topico/48806/problemas-na-tematica.
3 BoardGameGeek. 2020. "History and Theme Question". Forums. Accessed December 21, 2022. https://boardgamegeek.com/thread/2542327/history-and-theme-question/page/1.
4 This image of Dom Pedro II, Colonial Brazil and of the Imperial period is a recurrent theme in Brazilian TV shows and *telenovelas,* such as *Nos Tempos do Imperador* (In the Times of the Emperor, Globo, 2021), *Novo Mundo* (New World, Globo, 2017) and *Sinhá Moça* (Little Missy, Globo, 2006).
5 The author, Zé Mendes, is affiliated with activist organizations that are part of the "monarchist movement", a collection of organized groups (Veleda, 2021) that ask for the re-institution of a parliamentary monarchy government in Brazil, with the return of the Brazilian imperial family into power (Confembras, n.d.).
6 Poder360. 2022. June 17. "Bolsonaro diz que ser presidente é "missão" de Deus". *Poder360,* June 17, 2022. https://www.poder360.com.br/governo/bolsonaro-diz-que-ser-presidente-e-missao-de-deus/.
7 Reuters. 2018. October 6. "Bolsonaro diz defender país de comunismo e "curar" lulistas com trabalho". *Exame,* October 6, 2018. https://exame.com/brasil/bolsonaro-diz-defender-pais-de-comunismo-e-curar-lulistas-com-trabalho/.
8 https://ludopedia.com.br/topico/48806/problemas-na-tematica?id_topico=48806& unread=true&pagina=1#id_post_0
9 Quilombos are small, self-managed communities that were usually formed by enslaved people in Colonial Brazil to escape from slavery and perform their own cultural identity (Vaz, 2016).

References – books and articles

Arantes, Pedro Fiori, and Cláudio Ribeiro Rezende. 2023. "Western Fantasy and Tropical Nightmare: Spectacular Architecture and Urban Warfare in Rio." In *The Routledge Handbook of Architecture, Urban Space and Politics, Volume I*, edited by Nikolina Bobic and Farzaneh Haghighi. London: Routledge.

Booth, Paul. 2021. *Boardgames as Media*. London: Bloomsbury Academic.

Borit, Cornel, Melania Borit, and Petter Olsen. 2018. "Representations of Colonialism in Three Popular, Modern Board Games: Puerto Rico, Struggle of Empires, and Archipelago." *Open Library of Humanities*, 4: 1–40. https://doi.org/10.16995/olh.211.

Boym, Svetlana. 2001. *The Future of Nostalgia*. New York, NY: Basic Books.

Brown, Wendy. 2019. *In the Ruins of Neoliberalism: The Rise of Antidemocratic Politics in the West*. New York, NY: Columbia University Press.

Confembras. n.d. "A Confembras." Accessed December 18, 2022. https://www.movimentomonarquista.com.br/a-confembras/.

Coontz, Stephanie. 2000. *The Way We Never Were: American Families and the Nostalgia Trap*. New York, NY: Basic Books.

Covil dos Jogos. 2020. "Papo do Ladino e Bloco do Block: Resenha Brazil: Imperial." Accessed December 18, 2022. https://covildosjogos.com.br/2021/04/18/papo-do-ladino-e-bloco-do-block-resenha-brazil-imperial/.

Eco, Umberto. 1986. *Travels in Hyperreality: Essays*. San Diego, CA: Harcourt Brace & Company.

Falcão, Thiago, Daniel Marques, and Ivan Mussa. 2020a. "#BoycottBlizzard: Capitalismo de Plataforma e a Colonização do Jogo." *Revista Contracampo – Brazilian Journal of Communication*, 39. https://doi.org/10.22409/contracampo.v0i0.38578.

Falcão, Thiago, Daniel Marques, Ivan Mussa, and Tarcizio Macedo. 2020b. "At the Edge of Utopia. Esports, Neoliberalism and the Gamer Culture's Descent into Madness." *Gameviroments*, 13: 382–419. https://doi.org/10.26092/elib/411.

Falcão, Thiago, Tarcizio Macedo, and Gabriela Kurtz. 2021. "Conservadorismo E Masculinidade tóxica Na Cultura Gamer: Uma aproximação a Magic: The Gathering." *MATRIZes*, 15(2): 251–277. https://doi.org/10.11606/issn.1982-8160.v15i2p251-277.

Fedriga, Ricardo. 2021. "Dystopias and Historiographical Objects: The Strange Case of The Middle Ages." *Rivista di estetica*, 76: 60–75.

Foasberg, Nancy. 2016. "The Problematic Pleasures of Productivity and Efficiency in Goa and Navegador." *Analog Game Studies*, 3(1). https://analoggamestudies.org/volume-iii-issue-i/

Harvey, David. 2005. *A Brief History of Neoliberalism*. New York, NY: Oxford University Press.

Iamamoto, Sue A. S., Maíra Kubík Mano and Renata Summa. 2021. "Brazilian Far-Right Neoliberal Nationalism: Family, Anti-Communism and the Myth of Racial Democracy." *Globalizations*. https://doi.org/10.1080/14747731.2021.1991745.

Kurtz, Gabriela. 2019. ""Respeita aí": os discursos e a subversão das regras como manifestações de violência simbólica de gênero nos jogos digitais Dota 2 e League of Legends." PhD diss., Universidade Federal do Rio Grande do Sul.

Latour, Bruno. 2002. "Morality and Technology: The End of the Means." *Theory Culture & Society*, 19(5–6): 247–260. https://doi.org/10.1177/026327602761899246.

88   *T. Falcão and A. Carneiro*

Ludopedia. n.d. "Brazil: Imperial." Accessed December 18, 2021. https://ludopedia.com.br/jogo/brazil-imperial.

Mbembe, Achille. 2019. *Necropolitics*. Durham, NC: Duke University Press.

MeepleBR. n.d. "Brazil: Imperial + Extras." Accessed December 18, 2021. https://www.lojameeplebrjogos.com.br/brazil-imperial-extras.

Messias, José Carlos. 2016. "Saudações do Terceiro Mundo": games customizados, gambiarra e habilidades cognitivas na cultura hacker." PhD diss., Universidade Federal do Rio de Janeiro.

Mignolo, Walter. 1991. *The Idea of Latin America*. Hoboken, NJ: Wiley-Blackwell Press.

Mukherjee, Souvik. 2018. "Playing Subaltern: Video Games and Postcolonialism." *Games and Culture*, 13(5): 504–520. https://doi.org/10.1177/1555412015627258.

Muñoz, Andreas Bijsterveld. 2022. "National Identity in Historical Video Games: An Analysis of How Civilization V Represents the Past." *Nations and Nationalism*, 28(4): 1311–1325. https://doi.org/10.1111/nana.12845.

Penix-Tadsen, Phillip. 2019. *Cultural Code: Video Games and Latin America*. Cambridge, MA: MIT Press.

Pullen, Nick. 2018. "Colonialism is Fun? Sid Meier's Civilization and the Gamification of Imperialism." *Imperial & Global Forum*, July 3, 2018. https://imperialglobalexeter.com/2018/07/03/colonialism-is-fun-sid-meiers-civilization-and-the-gamification-of-imperialism/.

Salles, Ricardo. 2013. *Nostalgia Imperial: escravidão e formação da identidade nacional no Brasil do Segundo Reinado*. Rio de Janeiro: Editora Ponteio, 212p.

Salter, Anastasia, and Bridget Blodgett. 2017. *Toxic Geek Masculinity in Media: Sexism, Trolling, and Identity Policing*. London: Palgrave Macmillan.

Tábula Quadrada. 2022. "Brazil Imperial: overview em vídeo e review escrito." Accessed December 18, 2022. https://tabulaquadrada.com.br/brazil-imperial-overview-em-video-e-review-escrito/.

Tolotti, Rodrigo. December 3, 2022. "Mais que brincadeira de criança: vendas de jogos de tabuleiro disparam no Brasil, mas mercado tem grandes desafios." *InfoMoney*. https://www.infomoney.com.br/negocios/mais-que-brincadeira-de-crianca-vendas-de-jogos-de-tabuleiro-disparam-no-brasil-mas-mercado-tem-grandes-desafios/.

Trammell, Aaron. 2021. "Playing with Letters and Landscapes: Interacting with Empire in Early 19th Century Print Learning Aides." *Revista Contracampo – Brazilian Journal of Communication*, 40. https://doi.org/10.22409/contracampo.v40i2.51430.

Vaz, Beatriz Accioly. 2016. "Quilombos." In *Dicionário IPHAN de Patrimônio Cultural*, edited by Bettina Grieco et al. Rio de Janeiro: IPHAN/DAF/Copedoc.

Veleda, Raphael. February 24, 2021. "Participamos do encontro de jovens monarquistas e te contamos como foi." *Metrópoles*. https://www.metropoles.com/brasil/participamos-do-encontro-de-jovens-monarquistas-e-te-contamos-como-foi.

Woods, Stewart. 2012. *Eurogames: The Design, Culture and Play of Modern European Board Games*. Jefferson, NC: McFarland & Company.

Young, Helen Victoria. 2016. *Race and Popular Fantasy Literature: Habits of Whiteness*. London: Routledge.

Zapata, Beatriz Pérez. 2020. "Videojuegos poscoloniales. Jugar contra los otros, jugar a ser otros." In *Pensar el Juego: 25 Caminos para los Game Studies*, edited by Victor Navarro Remesal. Valencia: Shangrila.

References – games

Epic Games, Fortnite. Digital game, 2017.

Garena, Freefire. Digital game, 2017.

Kosmos, Settlers of Catan. Analog game designed by Klaus Teuber, 1995.

MeepleBR, Brazil: Imperial. Analog game designed by Zé Mendes, 2021.

MicroProse, Civilization. Digital game, 1991

Ravensburger, Puerto Rico. Analog game designed by Andreas Seyfarth, 2002.

Roblox Corporation, Roblox. Digital game, 2006.

7 Heritagization and Heritage Conflict

The Finnish *Afrikan tähti* Board Game and Its Change to Contested Heritage, 1951–2021

Anna Sivula

Jaakko Suominen

Introduction

A notable Finnish board game publisher Kuvataide released the *Afrikan tähti* (*The Star of Africa*) board game in 1951. The game was created by a young designer Kari Mannerla (1930–2006) who had just started his professional career in the advertising business. He had first developed the idea for the game in the late 1940s after experimenting with several other designs in the racing genre. The game board layout was a drawn map of the African continent with depictive elements inspired by colonial adventure stories, such as Edgar Rice Burroghs' *Tarzan* book series (1912–), as well as movies starring Humphrey Bogart, such as *Casablanca* (1942) and *African Queen* (1951). Most likely Mannerla got inspiration from some earlier games too even though not mentioned that. Players' objective was to discover the Star of Africa jewel and bring it back to the game's starting point, Cairo or Tangier. The game mechanics were novel and more complex than earlier dice-rolling racing games in Finland. The *Afrikan tähti* allowed for many possible travel routes and means of transportation. It also included turntable chips and play money.

The game became an unprecedented commercial success in Finland. According to its later publisher Peliko, *Afrikan tähti* sales reached a total of hundred thousand copies by 1957, one million by 1986 and four million by 2013 (e.g., Eronen 2000; Mannerla 2013). The first version for a foreign market was published in Norway in 1956, and after that, *Afrikan tähti* became popular also in other Nordic countries. Over the years it has been marketed across Europe, as well as in English-speaking countries worldwide but its international success has been rather modest outside of the Nordic region. By the 1980s, *African tähti* was one of the most recognized board games in Finland, along

DOI: 10.4324/9781003356318-7

with international hits such as *Monopoly* or *Trivial Pursuit*. Interestingly, it was the first board game in Finland to have a licensed computer game port, released for Commodore 64 in 1985. However, this digital version developed by one of the pioneers of the Finnish video game industry – Amersoft, was a commercial failure (Pasanen and Suominen 2018).

Undoubtedly, *African tähti* has been recognized as one of the most successful Finnish board games. However, at the same time, it has evoked more and more public debate related to its depiction of Africa which is claimed to be colonialist, imperialist, and lately, even racist. In this chapter, we study closely the *heritagization* process of *Afrikan tähti* and address the following research questions. How did it become a board game classic in Finland? How did the public reception of the game change over the seven decades? Subsequently, how did it become a subject of antiracist and postcolonial academic discussions? And finally, did this *cultural heritage conflict* affect *African tähti*'s status as valuable heritage, shifting it toward nonvaluable heritage (on value creation see Wieland et al. 2016)?

We argue that questioning and contesting of *Afrikan tähti's* heritage value has taken place in several intensifying waves, starting already in the late 1990s. These waves have been connected to the multiculturalization of Finland, ongoing historical changes in academic and public debates, lately also in social media, as well as cultural shifts in usage, production, value and meaning-making processes related to the institutionalization of games in general.

The chapter consists of six sections. Firstly, we introduce our theoretical approach. Then we examine in chronological order the waves of the *Afrikan tähti* heritagization process. In the last section, we discuss the game as a contested heritage object.

As a theoretical concept, contested heritage has been used already more than 20 years, but rarely exactly defined, or applied in the Nordic or game cultural context with historical case studies. In many cases, the concept has been connected with another term, dissonant heritage, but according to Liu et al. (2021), contested heritage is understood usually more neutral and broader compared to dissonant heritage where case studies focus typically on negative or unwanted heritage. Liu et al. also note that contestation of heritage stems from the change of time as well as "every step of heritagization may lead to its contestation" (450). All of these can be seen in the case of the *Afrikan tähti*.

Our primary sources for public discourse analysis of *Afrikan tähti* heritagization process consist of newspaper and magazine articles on the game published since the early 1990s. We use the online archive of *Helsingin Sanomat*, the biggest newspaper in Finland, as well as its publisher Sanoma's online repository that includes materials circulated, for example in the popular tabloid *Ilta-Sanomat*. We have also used a newspaper article collection made available by the publisher of *Afrikan tähti* and preserved by the Finnish Museum of Games. The newspaper and magazine material offers if not a complete, at least a *comprehensive picture* of changes in public discourses. In addition to that, we have investigated online news, popular blog posts and existing research literature on *Afrikan tähti*.

Critical Cultural Heritage Studies as Theoretical Framework

Our theoretical framework is based on critical cultural heritage studies. We approach cultural heritage as continuous and dissonant interaction of bottom-up consumer culture and top-down Authorized Heritage Discourse (AHD). (On the dissonance of game cultural heritage see Mochocki 2021, 82. On AHD, see Smith 2006, 4; 2021,47, 57–61). As Mochocki crystallizes: "Heritage is dissonant. It is a constitutive social process that on the one hand is about regulating and legitimizing, and on the other hand is about working out, contesting and challenging a range of cultural and social identities, sense of place, collective memories, values and meanings that prevail in the present and can be passed to the future." (Mochocki 2021, 82).

AHD is no longer considered to be dictated by the State, but as a (contesting) dialogue of top-down and bottom-up cultural heritage discourse. The dissonant nature of *heritagization,* the becoming of a heritage, is the profound cause of the escalating heritage conflicts.

The concept of heritagization was originally coined by Robert Hewison in his book *The Heritage Industry: Britain in a Climate of Decline* (1987), in which he refers to the cultural heritage process of certain spatial sites. Since Hewison, the notion has often referred to a *meaning-making process of local or spatial objects or practices.* Heritagization was also, in the early 1990s, understood in terms of the cultural production of a represented past (Walsh 1992). The concept of heritagization, as a process of an object or site transforming to heritage, is dominating the content of David Lowenthal's *Possessed by the Past: The Heritage Crusade and the Spoils of History*, which enlightens, in 1996, how heritage and the use of histories became a source of present conflicts. Rodney Harrison (2013, 4–5), in his turn, represents the next generation, emphasizing the positive creative power of heritage as a tool for shaping the future.

Heritagization is a process maintained by a community. (Smith 2006, 2021; Poria 2010; Sivula 2015). According to Regina Bendix (2009), heritagization refers to the elevation of particular, selected objects or practices to be preserved the future generations of the more or less imagined community, such as a nation-state, or mankind. Heritagization is carried on by a complicated mishmash of different, local, national, translocal or international meaning-makers: owners, users, buyers, sellers, practitioners, experts, audiences and state officials. Heritagization can be approached as a changing emotional attachment between the *heritage-as-a-thing* and the possessive subjects or groups, who claim rights over objects or practices they value as their heritage (Coombe 1998, 2013; Smith 2021).

The notion of heritagization is widely used in the field of critical heritage studies, especially referring to the national or regional processes that are related to the meaning-making process of spatial or historical traces of the past. The French notion of *patrimonialisation* (Isnart 2012; Mauz 2012, Salemnic 2016) refers to the *making of heritage.* The process of heritagization can be defined as the making of heritage – *that* is what the heritagization is about.

A case study of a heritage conflict of the *Afrikan tähti* game helps us to understand the dynamics of cultural heritage. Things may have been considered as a legacy by a group of people from one generation to the other, but the label of heritage involves claims by others for recognition of such legacy having an extraordinary value which may be local, national or global (Salemnic 2016, 316–319).

Heritagization is a functional socio-cultural process of the identification of cultural heritage and creation of cultural heritage value. Cultural heritage is therefore not an object, e.g., a game, but a process, maintained by an identity-working heritage community (Smith 2006, 4 and 82; 2021, 76–78; Waterton and Watson 2015, 7). The identity work of a community can be observed in three different forms: *possessive, historicizing and monumentalizing* (Sivula 2015, 64) (See Fig. 7.1).

The clash of identity work may occur if two or more heritage communities are heritagizing the same cultural heritage object. Historicizing identity work takes place, when a heritage community produces a sense of belonging, a participant experience to a shared history. Monumentalizing identity work derives from the encountering of shared history (of a heritage community) and the tangible or intangible "things" that might be considered as evidence of the history. Possessive identity work consists of the heritage communities effort of appropriating the material and immaterial evidence of the community's own past.

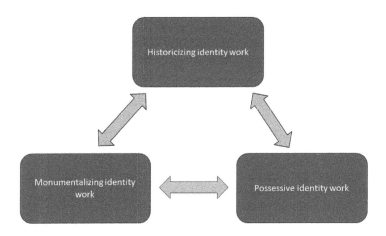

Figure 7.1 Three Forms of Communal Identity Work by Sivula (2015)

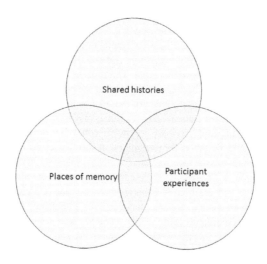

Figure 7.2 Components of Heritological Identity Work by Sivula (2015)

To put it short, the components of a successful heritological identity work and a functioning culture heritage community are (1) a place of memory (a heritage object), (2) history shared by and within a community, and (3) a participant experience (Fig. 7.2).

The active heritage community is located in the intersection of these three components, and it exists only as long as the threefold identity work continues. The symbolic or even real value of a heritage is created by an identity-working cultural heritage community.

A heritage community is a community of consumers. It can, as we have proven in the case of Finnish Museum of Games (see Suominen et al. 2018), be observed as a community that willingly invests money in the heritagization of game culture. The community of investors is not only imagined, as Anderson (1991) puts it, but also very real, realistic and tangible. AHD is remarkably involved with the value creation of tangible commodities.

Value creation is, however, a twofold process. The value of heritage is not only added in the process, but it might as well be removed, especially in heritage conflicts. In heritage conflict, the identity work takes a dysfunctional form. In sociology, the "dysfunctional" refers to any action or behavior that has negative consequences for a group or society; an effect of structures that fosters social instability (https://sociologydictionary.org/dysfunction/). The functional is an opposite type of action and behavior.

The dysfunctional, counter identity work confronts the above-mentioned normal and functional forms of identity work. The heritage conflict can be observed as *alienating, abasing* and *rejective* identity work (Sivula 2017,

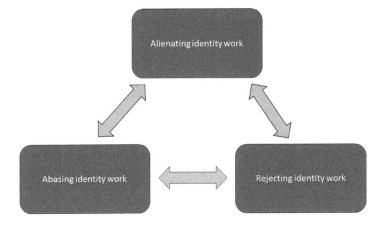

Figure 7.3 Functional Forms of Identity Work by Sivula (2015).

316–317) (See Fig. 7.3). In this chapter, we examine the emergence, inter-action and co-construction of game cultural heritage from the point of view of both functional and dysfunctional forms of identity work.

A Politicized Game Board

As we stated above, *Afrikan tähti* game had become a Finnish board game classic by the 1980s. The classic status was based on the game's long-term and continuous popularity. The classic was not the only one of its kind. Similar Finnish classics were e.g., the *Kimble* game (1967) published by Nelostuote. It was based on the concept of an American game *Trouble*.

Afrikan tähti was a peculiar Finnish board game also because its designer Kari Mannerla was mentioned on the cover of the game and on the board. Mannerla actively influenced new versions of the game, rule changes and licensing. He also actively promoted the game in public. Mannerla's personal role as a promoter of his creation increased from the 1990s onwards (see, e.g., Mannerla 1997).

In 1992, the intellectual property rights for *Afrikan tähti* were transferred to Peliko Oy. In 1995, *Helsingin Sanomat* reported that Peliko had started sponsoring Finland's first black football team, because the team had chosen the name F.C. African Star (Pasanen 1995). The cultural tolerance of the time was different from the current. The football team was first sponsored by the confectionery manufacturer Fazer, whose licorice bars were distributed by the players before the match and the team's Finnish manager called the distribution to "black humor of the black men" in the interview by *Helsingin Sanomat*. The wrappers of the bars, introduced already several decades earlier, were decorated with an extremely exaggerated and stereotypical drawing of a dark-skinned person. It was as late as in 2008 that the racist imagery paper wrapping caused some image problems to Fazer, which the company tried to solve. After the wrapper had been publicly discussed even abroad, Fazer changed the decoration of the lollipop bar to a black and red pepper. The racist imagery was not believed to strengthen the export of the company and the company got rid of the notorious images that Leena-Maija Rossi calls representations of imagery of visual colonialism. (Rossi 2009. On Fazer case, see also Korhonen 2008).

The number of African immigrants in Finland had started to increase in the early 1990s, when refugees in particular from Somalia had come to Finland. At the beginning of the 1990s, the national economy of Finland was in recession, and the arrival of refugees aroused opposition and apparently racist attitudes toward the Somali refugees (Pirkkalainen et al. 2016, 70). However, the *Afrikan tähti* game was still not yet widely viewed from the perspective of *dark heritage*, although the terms of dark heritage, *dissonant heritage, contested heritage* and *negative heritage*, have appeared recently in heritological discussions. Unlike negative heritage, dark heritage is a functional form of heritage and a raw material of cultural production. The term refers most often to the touristic sites with a grim history: a concentration camp, a battlefield or the surroundings of Chernobyl (Rico 2008; Thomas et al. 2019).

More attention was paid to another game with racist imagery. The *Musta Pekka* (*Black Peter*) card game was known in many countries at the beginning of the 19th century. The name of the game had already been changed to Pekka in Finland probably in the late 1980s. Despite the name change, the old racist illustration of the game continued to exist, which sparked a debate in the public and time and again the game was demanded to be banned as racist. However, in the debate of *Musta Pekka* there was no reference to the *Afrikan Tähti*. Peliko was also the manufacturer of the *Pekka* game. Publisher of *Pekka*, then Martinex company, took the game out of production in 2020 after the public debate (Tahkokorpi 2020).

"National taste" was referred to in 1995, when Peliko launched a new de luxe version of the *Afrikan tähti* game. In the new version, the renewed board was apparently based on the Swedish version. The native figures and the animals no longer looked the same as before. *Helsingin Sanomat* complained that the new version was developed worse (*Helsingin Sanomat kuukausiliite* 12/1995). Apparently, the original cheaper version still sold better than the de luxe version at the time.

The two earliest Finnish research publications, which dealt critically with imperialism and colonialism in the *Afrikan tähti*, were published in 1997. Their authors were scholars of comparative literature at the University of Tampere. They analyzed the game as a text and dealt with the representations of Africa in the pictures. They did not, however, analyze, for example, the players' perspective or the reception of the game. Juri Nummelin's (1997) essay only dealt with the game, but Olli Löytty placed in his book *Afrikan tähti* in the context of colonialist African literature. Löytty (1997, 13–14) wrote: "Tarzan is one example of how boys' adventure literature has shaped our image of Africa. Likewise, the *Afrikan tähti* is not an 'innocent' pastime, but an active 'storyteller' that repeats and renews the many myths about Africa from the colonial era. The very purpose of the game, i.e. 'to search for the Star of Africa by land, sea and air and bring it to a safe place', as the rules of the game say, tells what colonialism is all about. The plot is like straight from the history of colonialism: On the game board you can find the Gold Coast, where you can get double the price of a jewel, the Slavery Coast, where the player may have to remain a slave, and the Sahara desert, where you may be delayed by a Bedouin attack."

Leila Koivunen and Anna Rastas, who write about the academic history of Finnish postcolonialism studies, state (2020, 430) that the discipline of comparative literature was more active than other academic disciplines in the bringing of the postcolonial discussions to Finland. According to them, postcolonial research literature first came naturally to those disciplines that studied former colonies or diaspora cultures connected to colonialism. There was a considerable amount of such research in the field of literary studies. Another key factor was the trending cultural studies approach in the University of Tampere's literary studies, which was represented by Dr. Mikko Lehtonen and his students – who were responsible for these *Afrikan tähti* references. The theories related to Stuart Hall's concept of identity had been discussed in Finland, and Stuart Hall's writings were also translated into Finnish in the late 1990s. The position of postcolonial theory was also strengthened at the intersections of feminist research and the research of developing countries. (Koivunen and Rastas 2020, 431.)

The critical interpretations of the *Afrikan tähti* did not receive special attention outside the universities, with one exception. Historian Erkki Vetten-niemi, who had published studies on sports and dealt with questions of other social issues, criticized and parodied the texts of Löytty and Nummelin in his column "Slave Coast Prisoners" ("Orjarannikon vangit") in *Helsingin Sano-mat*. Vetenniemi lampooned the academic style of the authors: "In otherwise entertaining criticism, the omniscient and therefore arrogant attitude of its presenters is suspect. [...] I claim that Cairo and Tangier represent the Orient in the game's discursive world, the intermediate space between barbarism and civilization, where the player retreats before the next penetration into the Negroid Otherness." (Vetenniemi 1998.)

The tip of the criticism was therefore aimed especially at the way of speaking of the researchers, which was characterized as arrogant and alienated from (the people's) reality. As a result, the researchers' discourse was labeled as entertaining at best. However, the discussion implicitly built a connection to the earlier uproar about popular culture, the (late) 1970s debate about the *Donald Duck* comics and the Walt Disney Company. In its most stripped-down form, the *Donald Duck* debate focused on the comic's immorality, because the Ducks had no pants, but yet, it was more about Marxist criticism directed at *Donald Duck* as a pusher and spreader of capitalist and imperialist values.

The work *How to Read Donald Duck* (published originally in Chile in 1971 with the name *Para leer al Pato Donald* and translated in English in 1975) by the Argentine-Chilean novelist, activist and scholar Ariel Dorfman and the Belgian sociologist Armand Mattelart had been translated to Finnish in 1980, and the criticism (and the criticism of the criticism) were rampant, e.g., around this work. On the one hand, Vetteniemi's critique of criticism refers to the idea that one cannot look for very deep political meanings in the products of popular culture, but on the other hand, it reminds us that these products can be considered so untouchable that their value should not be questioned. An abasive act toward a popular cultural heritage is often a source of an intentional or unintentional conflict (Sivula 2017).

In general, these writings received very little attention. At the turn of the millennium, the *Afrikan tähti* was in the public eye mainly via the announcements of new game versions, such as the card game and the scratch cards, and also in situations where the game's continuous steady sales and status as a classic were emphasized. Articles about the game were also published in two collecting magazines, which also revealed the game's status as a classic (Simula 1998; Eronen 2000). Nevertheless, the next discursive turn took place shortly after the turn of the millennium.

From Anniversary Celebrations to the Second Wave of Criticism

In 2001, the *Afrikan tähti* turned 50. For the anniversary, a festive version of the game, a puzzle, and other special versions of the *Afrikan tähti* were released. The journalists interviewed the game's designer, Kari Mannerla, and for example, an article in the *Helsingin Sanomat* discussed widely the cultural context of the game's date of birth and the limited knowledge of Africa in Finland at the time (Santajärvi 2002). The board game was thus considered to have aroused many players' interest in Africa. The game had inspired players to find out more about the countries and cultures of the African continent. There was no especially critical cultural heritage discourse in the articles, and the articles did not carry out abasing identity work. The game was still monumentalized by the game cultural heritage community.

In terms of racism, another Finnish consumer product that has become iconic attracted attention that year. Confectionery company Brunberg produced cream-filled chocolate sweets whose German-derived name used the n-word and referred to kissing, in Finnish "Neekerinpusu". The candy packaging had a stereotypical image of a kissing dark-skinned couple. Due to the discussion and, for example, negative international attention, Brunberg short-ened the name of its product to a "kiss", and changed the package decoration a little. However, the picture of a kissing dark-skinned couple was removed and replaced with a drawn landscape picture of Porvoo's old town only in the summer of 2020.(*Ilta-Sanomat* May 16, 2001; Salokorpi 2020).

The individual examples concerning products and product packaging show that consumer culture had changed, and the producers reacted. Criticism of colonialism and racism have begun to enter into public discussion in the realm of Finnish consumer culture at the beginning of the 2000s. However, the discussion did not directly usually use academic concepts such as com-modity racism that refers to the circulation of colonial views and images with various consumer products, packaging, and in advertising (McClintock 1995. See also Rossi 2009; Purtschert et al. 2016).

In 2003, the immaterial property rights to *Afrikan tähti* were trans-ferred to the Martinex company. Another important year in the game's history at the beginning of the 2000s was the year 2005. That's when the game's creator, Kari Mannerla, turned 75. The birthday interview referred, among other things, to the critical discussion about the game. According to the 75th birthday interview (STT): "Kari Mannerla is clearly a bit an-noyed that Afrikan Tähti has been given a colonialist label in some recent reviews. – It is worth remembering that those African countries were colonies in the 1950s. You could say that if I realize my idea of a game set on the planet Mars, it will also be a colonialist game one day. Mannerla still insists that the Afrikan tähti has never been accused of being racist." (*Turun Sanomat* September, 21, 2005.)

The following year Mannerla died and the obituaries discussed, among other things, the cultural meaning of the *Afrikan tähti*. Mannerla had become Finland's most famous board game designer. Game was also introduced in *100 Social Innovations from Finland* book with other things such as sauna, Linux operating system, maternity pack, Finland's Slot Machine Association, Molotov cocktail incendiary weapon, and many more. Likewise, several *Afri-kan tähti* world championships competitions were organized in Helsinki since 2005. All of that showed game's increased cultural legacy.

After Mannerla's death, the critical discussion about the *Afrikan tähti* began to expand, but was still not very large-scale. On October 28, 2006, the tabloid *Ilta-Sanomat* published a short article with the title "African star imperialism!" In the story, Marianne Peltomaa was interviewed. She was in-troduced as a writer and the mother of two children adopted from Colombia. She had previously written an opinion piece on the subject, and *Ilta-Sanomat* was clearly digging up a selling confrontation. The reporter asked questions about the game's racism and racism in general, and Peltomaa answered them:

- "I think the game is not racist, but it has a conqueror context. The question arises, what kind of images the game leaves behind, Peltomaa ponders.

Well, what kind? What kind of effects do you think playing for the Afrikan tähti can have on children?

* These are dangerous questions, Peltomaa laughs.
* The effects are not clear-cut, and I don't think that this board game should be banned. But it would be important to discuss these questions and thus raise people's awareness."

Game expert Dr. Jyrki Kasvi was also interviewed in the *Ilta-Sanomat*. He too stated that the game is colonialist, as was the mental atmosphere in Finland during the time when the board game was designed.

In 2007, "the Star of Africa – the flip side of the game board" exhibition was opened at the Helinä Rautavaara Anthropological Museum in Espoo, a museum that presents the diverse cultures of the world. The museum's own collection of objects was based on materials collected by Rautavaara, who traveled around the world. In the museum's exhibition, the *Afrikan tähti* board game was used as a springboard for the treatment of Africa in the same way as Olli Löytty's book *Valkoinen pimeys* (*White Darkness*) (1997). A book was also published about the exhibition, written by social anthropologist and Africanist Katja Uusihakala (2007). Likewise, the exhibition that was circulated in other museums and supported by the Ministry of Foreign Affairs' international education project, somewhat fueled the discussion about the colonial nature of the *Afrikan tähti* game. Pia Laine presented the exhibition in *Maailman Kuvalehti* (published by the Finnish Development NGOs Fingo association) and also in *Kumppani* magazine. Although the article brought up the connection of the game to the colonialist thinking of the time of its birth, the magazine also went through how the exhibition had been able to utilize people's nostalgic attitude toward the game. Thus, by using elements of the game board in the exhibition, the exhibition expanded their images and perceptions of the different dimensions of Africa (Laine 2007). The attitude toward the game was, in these writings, still quite neutral and reflected the understanding of different contexts and interpretation frameworks of an artefacta.

The conversation continued a couple of years later. For example, Hannu Salmi, professor of cultural history, who had extensively studied the history of media and popular culture, referred in his newspaper column and blog post to the contradictions of the *Afrikan tähti*, which actually do not allow any one-sided colonialist interpretation of the game. Salmi wrote: "Realists could argue that Afrikan tähti is a colonialist game because the players are only there to gather natural resources. Undoubtedly, the game carries with it a colonial legacy, but on the other hand, the bandits in the game also do look European. After all, is there a big difference between the players and the western-style robbers loitering on the game board?" (Salmi 2009.)

The Escalation of the Heritage Conflict

Temporal milestones, for example, the milestones of 10, 50, and 100 years of history, and the celebrations of anniversaries, have an accelerating effect to the heritagization of a thing. (Sivula 2015). The life of the board game continued in the 2010's. In 2011 the 60th anniversary edition of *Afrikan tähti* was released. At least the word celebration was written on the cover of the box. In 2013 Martinex released also a free mobile plugin for *Afrikan tähti*, and in 2014 a game supplement "Retkikunnat" (Expeditions) was published (Saari 2014).

Anne-Marie Lindfors mentioned briefly *Afrikan tähti* game in her doctoral dissertation on West African Novels in Finnish Translation in 2015 when she wrote about the history of representations of Africa for Finnish children. Lindfors referred to the previous Löytty's study (1997) and claimed that the game "repeats many colonial myths about Africa and its exploitation". Likewise, cultural historian Henna Ylänen (2017) referred to *Afrikan tähti*'s colonial representations in her article on nationalism in the early Finnish board games.

In 2017 the heritagization of the *Afrikan tähti* culminated, when the historical artifacta entered in a museum. The board game was selected to be displayed in the new Finnish Museum of Games, which was opened in Tampere. Several versions of the game were – and still are in 2022 – on display in the museum. In the Finnish Museum of Games the game was first presented as follows: "Afrikan Tähti ('The Star of Africa') is a Finnish classic and a game experience that brings generations together. Designed by Kari Mannerla when he was 19 years old, Afrikan Tähti has been translated into 16 languages and it has sold over 3.6 million copies – half of them internationally. The game was inspired by Humphrey Bogart's films and the fascinating names on a crumpled map of Africa – not so much by the reality of Africa. Over the years, the game has been criticized for its colonial view of the world." The introductory text was slightly changed in 2022 for recognizing even more clearly the recent critical discussion. Also in the early 2000s, the game was placed in critical context in a small museum of Finnish-African cultural center Villa Karo in Grand-Popo, Benin.

In the spring of 2021, the 70th-anniversary version of the *Afrikan tähti* was released, with a new graphic outfit designed by Matti Pikkujämsä. Some colonial or otherwise contradictory elements were removed from the new outfit (e.g., bandits replaced by panthers), but the new graphics raised some debate if the changes spoiled the classic. The publisher of the game, Martinex, announced that four daughters of the original designer Kari Mannerla had overseen the graphic modification (Kilpamäki 2021). A wooden special edition of the game was also released in the same year.

In 2021 the heritage conflict of the *Afrikan tähti* escalated in the University of Helsinki. The new controversy was related to the processing of the game in a student happening of the freshman students of geography at the University.

Students had been dressed inspired by games and one group selected *Afrikan tähti* as their team and dressed as game's pawns, thieves, and diamonds. A German exchange student was shocked by the event that the person considered racist and reported it on social media. According to the newspapers, the exchange student wrote: "–The game describes European colonialism and people play it and raise their children like to end to act racist. The game does not only show how we have to contest Scandinavian participation to colonialism, but it also shows how there racist structures have been normalized in our societies when the children play it and the students use it with pleasure as 'fun game' when they introduce the campus area and the city for the new students" (e.g., Kuuskoski 2021).

The student union reacted quickly on social media and apologized that its activities were not "antiracist enough". The information on the case spread to newspapers that first reported it briefly and then started to write longer cover stories with interviews with African–Finnish activists and publicly known figures, representatives of the University of Helsinki, postcolonial researchers and others (e.g., *Yle News* October 20, 2021). In the comment sections on the newspapers, columns as well as on social media there were debates on the racism of the game and its classic status. Many people defended the game and considered the public debate overreaction. University of Helsinki for its part, organized crisis help for the shocked students, as well as anti-racism education.

Even before the situation, several scholars, coming from the postcolonial and antiracist studies, questioned the value of *African tähti* and referred to its racist and colonial nature (see e.g., Harrer and Laiti 2021; Harrer and Harviainen 2022). That was the first time when actual game studies scholars started to analyze the game more deeply and from the postcolonial point of view. Their research approach was based mostly in (cultural) game studies adopting various perspectives on intersectionality and postcolonial theory. Postcolonial game studies analyze not only colonial representations, simulations and cartographies in games but also games' various roles in colonial activities and maintaining their legacy as well gaming practices with ethnographic methods (Mukherjee 2017; Mukherjee and Hammar 2018 and the whole *Postcolonial Perspectives in Game Studies* theme issue of Open library of humanities, 2018).

Cultural heritage status of the *Afrikan tähti* has strengthened, but at the same time, its questioning has strengthened in another heritage community. Dark heritage of one heritage community may appear as a negative heritage of another heritage community. A mutual co-existence of two different heritage communities is enabled by the identification and avoidance of the dysfunctional forms of identity work, in both heritage communities (Sivula 2017). The reputation of a classic and the related discourse still lives on and creates tension between the horrified postcolonists, monumentalizing members of a game cultural heritage community, and the game historians, who try to contextualize the object and understand, what has thing been during its life, and how we can understand it in the changing contexts of cultural history. Like all heritage, dark heritage is polysemous and multivocal. It is important to note and reflect on different perspectives on dark heritage that heritage professionals and other interest groups, including researchers themselves, may have. (Thomas et al. 2019). It seems that the debate of the *Afrikan tähti* goes on, but the debaters are unable to communicate with each other. The debate has become heated especially on social media that is also fueled by tabloids and other press coverage.

Conclusion

Finnish historians Rinna Kullaa and her associates state (2022, 5–7) that Finland and Finns have a complicated relationship to colonialism. For a long time, colonialism has not been seen as an issue in Finland, because Finland had not been an imperialist global power, but rather a border region and object of exploitation for Russia and Sweden. Many academic and nonacademic Finns still deny that Finns could have been colonial actors. This attitude is visible in the debate about *Afrikan tähti* described in this chapter. However, according to Kullaa et al., many Finns have been in the service of colonial empires at different times, and colonialist ways of thinking have shaped Finnish culture and science as well as cultural products. Finns have also had several apparently colonialist projects in Lapland in the 20th century, and, especially during the Second World War, in other border regions. Merivirta et al. (2021, 6) also approach colonialism in a wider context, as cultural colonialism, and they argue that Finns' involvement in colonialism has taken place mostly at homes, in everyday situations. They note that "Finns circulated, shared, adopted, adapted, and created colonial discourses: texts, scientific studies, objects, imagery, and artifacts".

Finnish discussion, described in the chapter, has shown that Finnish colonialist mentality can be seen for example, in the *Afrikan tähti*, in the way that Finnishness is mirrored through strange and exotic foreign things. The purpose of this chapter has been to describe and analyze the cultural-historical process and the development of academic discussions that have shaped this postcolonialist situating of the *Afrikan tähti* in Finland. We have reflected the development of the discourse to another process, through which the *Afrikan tähti* game has become a cultural heritage object. When these two different discourses have met, a conflict circling around identity work have arose.

It takes history to locate the time, where a change and encounters emerged. The case of the Finland's first black football team F.C. African Star, in 1995, reveals a case of functional identity work and a playful example of shared heritage, which might be worth of further research. But did we, during our journey in history, find any traces of alienating, abasing and rejective identity work? Before the late 1990s there were none. On the contrary: There was a continuous, functional heritagization of the Finnish domestic practice of playing the contested game, which in 2017 finally led the thing to the Finnish Museum of Games, and definitely put located the *Afrikan tähti* under the heritage label. The first signs of dysfunctional identity work concerning the value of a game and the practice of playing it, appeared in the mid-1990s. A first public sign of an alienating identity work was actually introduced by Peliko in 1995: The referring to a "National taste" of Finnish players, and the renewing of the board were an attempt to disconnect the players from their historical practice of playing the game. The players, as consumers, resisted. In the same period, we find the first cultural signs of an abasing identity work, when the meaningfulness of *Afrikan tähti*, as a game cultural monument, seems to be devalorized by researchers. Again, the act evokes resistance in the heritage community. This time it occurred in a form of parody of a research article. These two discursive positions held their ground until a representation of the third form of dysfunctional identity work landed on the game cultural stage in 2021. This time it was a massive act of rejective identity work, reflecting the attempt to disturb the player cultural heritage community's sense of belonging. And again, there were signs of resistance, reflecting the awareness, but also the flexibility of a heritage community. The actual heritage conflict was solved in the University of Helsinki by a massive intervention, but as long as the discursive positions of this particular dysfunctional identity work are held, there is a heritage conflict. A counter-heritage community has emerged.

The *Afrikan tähti* game was born in 1951 in a society where *Casablanca* was shown in the movie theaters, and Tarzan was a young men's hero. *Afrikan tähti* survived, as a culturally active object. The playing of it was a practice, transmitted later from generation to generation. The game was time and again raised as an example of colonialism, and later, racism, but occasionally it was also defended by understanding of the cultural context of an artifacta. During the 2010s, *Afrikan tähti* was both heritagized and devalorized. The cultural history of this board game begs the question: Where is the thin line between a critical research-based discussion and dysfunctional identity work of a heritage community?

We argue that the story of the heritagization and negative heritagization of the Finnish board game *Afrikan tähti* reveals the need for a sense of the cultural-historical context of the game cultural, and historical objects.

People play games and join voluntarily in game cultural heritage communities. Likewise, historical games are played, and games are monumentalized as historical artifacts. The game cultural heritages are still under-represented on the World heritage lists. The domestic, ongoing practice of playing *Afrikan tähti* in Finland, is a good example of a nonlisted intangible game cultural heritage, transmitted from a generation to another. It is important to notice that people have a right to have nostalgia and personal value creation of cultural products they use and cherish. It takes, of course, cultural negotiations to accept, that one's dark heritage might be a negative heritage of another community. But, as long as no one gets hurt, both heritage communities are allowed to continue their own, functional identity work.

References

Anderson, Benedict. 1991. *Imagined Communities: Reflections on the Origin and Spread of Nationalism*. Revised and extended edition. London: Verso.

Coombe, Rosemary. 1998. *The Cultural Life of Intellectual Properties: Authorship, Appropriation, and the Law*. Durham, NC: Duke University Press.

Coombe, Rosemary. 2013. "Managing Cultural Heritage as Neoliberal Governmentality." In *Heritage Regimes and the State*, edited by Regina Bendix, Aditya Eggert, Arnkia Peselmann, and Sven Meßling, 375–387. Göttingen: University of Göttingen Press.

Dorfman, Ariel, and Armand Mattelart. 1980. *Kuinka Aku Ankkaa luetaan*. Originally in Spanish 1971 *Para leer al Pato Donald*. Translated in Finnish by Markku Koski. Helsinki: Love Kirjat.

Eronen, Esko. 2000. "Kaikki tähdestä. Afrikan tähti 1951–." *Keräilyn Maailma* 5/2000, 27–29.

Harrer, Sabine, and J. Tuomas Harviainen. 2022. "Where Are the White Perpetrators in All the Colonial Board Games? A Case Study on Afrikan Tähti." In *Representing Conflicts in Games*, edited by Jonas Linderoth, Björn Sjöblom, and Anders Frank, 171–187. London: Routledge.

Harrer, Sabine, and Outi Laiti. July 30, 2021. "Outside the Racist Nostalgia Box: Rethinking Afrikan tähti's Cultural Depictions." A paper presented in the Academic online seminar of Ropecon roleplaying convention.

Harrison, Rodney. 2013. *Heritage: Critical Approaches*. London: Routledge.

Helsingin Sanomat kuukausiliite 12/1995.

Hewison, Robert. 1987. *The Heritage Industry: Britain in a Climate of Decline*. London: Methuen.

Ilta-Sanomat. May 16, 2001. https://www.is.fi/kotimaa/art-2000000299441.html

Ilta-Sanomat. October 28, 2006. https://www.is.fi/kotimaa/art-2000000293735.html

Isnart, Cyril. 2012. "Les Patrimonialisations Ordinaires: Essai d'images Ethnographiées." *Ethnographiques*, vol. 24, Juillet. https://www.ethnographiques.org/2012/Isnart

Kilpamäki, Heini. April 15, 2021." Afrikan tähti uudistui – tältä näyttää uusi rosvo." *Iltalehti*. https://www.iltalehti.fi/kotimaa/a/d5346f32-8ef8-4969-ad9d-39c24544fc1a

Koivunen, Leila, and Anna Rastas. 2020. "Suomalaisen historiantutkimuksen uusi käänne? Kolonialismikeskustelujen kotouttaminen Suomea koskevaan tutkimukseen." *Historiallinen Aikakauskirja* 118 (4): 427–437.

Korhonen, Petri. February 29, 2008. "Cloetta Fazer posti lakupekan." *Taloussanomat*. https://www.is.fi/taloussanomat/art-2000001556265.html

Kullaa, Rinna, Janne Lahti, and Sami Lakomäki. 2022. "Esipuhe." In *Kolonialismi Suomen rajaseuduilla*, edited by Rinna Kullaa, Janne Lahdi, and Sami Lakomäki, 5–8. Helsinki: Gaudeamus.

Kuuskoski, Kaisla. October 18, 2021. "Afrikan tähti -pelistä räjähti rasismikohu Helsingin yliopistolla – opiskelijajärjestö pyytää anteeksi." *Ilta-Sanomat*. https://www.is.fi/kotimaa/art-2000008340694.html

Laine, Pia. December 3, 2007. "Afrikan tähden kääntöpuoli." *Maailman Kuvalehti.* https://maailmankuvalehti.fi/2007/12/pitkat/afrikan-tahden-kaantopuoli/

Lindfors, Anne-Marie. 2015. *West African Novels in Finnish Translation: Strategies for Africanised English.* PhD Dissertation. Helsinki: University of Helsinki, https://helda.helsinki.fi/handle/10138/153241.

Liu, Yang, Karine Dupre, and Xin Jin. 2021. "A Systematic Review of Literature on Contested Heritage." *Current Issues in Tourism* 24 (4): 442–465. https://doi.org/10.1080/13683500.2020.1774516

Löytty, Olli. 1997. *Valkoinen pimeys: Afrikka kolonialistisessa kirjallisuudessa.* Jyväskylä: Jyväskylän yliopisto.

Mannerla, Kari. February 20, 1997. "Afrikan tähden historia." Unpublished manuscript. Collection of Finnish Museum of Games.

Mannerla, Kari. 2013. "Star of Africa." In *100 Social Innovations from Finland*, edited by Ilkka Taipale, 347–351. Second Edition (First Edition 2006). Helsinki: Finnish Literature Society.

Mauz, Isabelle. 2012. "Les Justifications Mouvantes de la Patrimonialisation des Espèces 'Remarquables': L'exemple du Bouquetin des Alpes." *Ethnographiques* 24: 1–18.

McClintock, Anne. 1995. *Imperial Leather: Race, Gender and Sexuality in the Colonial Contest.* Abingdon: Routledge.

Merivirta, Raita, Leila Koivunen, and Timo Särkkä. 2021. "Finns in the Colonial World." In *Finnish Colonial Encounters: From Anti-Imperialism to Cultural Colonialism and Complicity*, edited by Raita Merivirta, Leila Koivunen, Timo Särkkä, 1–38. Cham: Springer.

Mochocki, Michał. 2021. *Role-Play as a Heritage Practice. Historical Larp, Tabletop RPG and Reenactment.* London: Routledge.

Mukherjee, Souvik. 2017. *Videogames and Postcolonialism: Empire Plays Back.* Cham: Springer.

Mukherjee, Souvik, and Emil Lundedal Hammar. 2018. "Introduction to the Special Issue on Postcolonial Perspectives in Game Studies." *Open Library of Humanities* 4 (2): 33. https://doi.org/10.16995/olh.309

Nummelin, Juri. 1997. "Imperialismin neljä unta ja painajainen: Afrikan tähden diskursiivisista muodostumista." *Kulttuurintutkimus* 14 (2): 34–40.

Pasanen, Esko. November 12, 1995. "'Afrikan tähti' tukee African Star -seuraa." *Helsingin Sanomat.*

Pasanen, Tero, and Jaakko Suominen. 2018. "Epäonnistunut yritys suomalaisen digitaalisen peliteollisuuden käynnistämiseksi: Amersoft 1984–1986." *Lähikuva* 31 (4): 27–47. https://journal.fi/lahikuva/article/view/77932

Pirkkalainen, Päivi, Hanna Wass, and Marjukka Weide. 2016." Suomen somalit osallistuvina kansalaisina." *Yhteiskuntapolitiikka* 81 (1): 69–77.

Poria, Yaniv. 2010. "The story behind the picture: Preferences for the visual display at heritage sites." In *Culture, heritage and representation: Perspectives on visuality and the past*, edited by Emma Waterton, and Steve Watson, 217–228. Surrey: Ashgate.

Purtschert, Patricia, Francesca Falk, and Barbara Lüthi. 2016. "Switzerland and 'Colonialism without Colonies'." *Interventions: International Journal of Postcolonial Studies* 18 (2): 286–302, https://doi.org/10.1080/1369801X.2015.1042395

Rico, Trinidad. 2008. "Negative Heritage: The Place of Conflict in World Heritage." *Conservation and Management of Archaeological Sites* 10 (4): 344–352. https://doi.org/10.1179/135050308X12513845914507

Rossi, Leena-Maija. 2009. "Licorice Boys and Female Coffee Beans: Representations of Colonial Complicity in Finnish Visual Culture." In *Complying with Colonialism*. *Gender, Race and Ethnicity in the Nordic Region*, edited by Suvi Keskinen, Salla Tuori, Sara Irni, and Diana Mulinari, 189–204. Abingdon: Ashgate.

Saari, Mikko. September 8, 2014. "Peliarvostelut: Afrikan tähti: Retkikunnat." *Lautapeliopas.* https://www.lautapeliopas.fi/peliarvostelut/afrikan-tahti-retkikunnat/

Salemnic, Oscar. 2016. "Described, Inscribed, Written Off: Heritagisation as (Dis)connection." In *Connected and Disconnected Vietnam: Remaking Social Relations in a Post-socialist Nation*, edited by Philip Taylor, 311–346. Canberra: ANU Press.

Salmi, Hannu. July 5, 2009. "Afrikan tähden salaisuus." *Hannu Salmen blogi.* http://hannusalmi.blogspot.com/2009/07/afrikan-tahden-salaisuus.html

Salokorpi, Jussi. March 2, 2020. "Brunbergin suukot uuteen pakettiin – suuteleva afrikkalaispari historiaan." *Yle.* https://yle.fi/uutiset/3-11236549

Santajärvi, Pirkko. February 14, 2002. "Tapasimme Kari Mannerlan. Afrikan Tähden lumo ei haihdu." *Helsingin Sanomat.* https://www.hs.fi/ihmiset/art-2000004031859.html

Simula, Timo. 1998. "Afrikan Tähti lumoaa sukupolvesta toiseen." *Keräilyharvinaisuus* 2/1998, 56–57.

Sivula, Anna. 2015. "Tilaushistoria identiteettityönä ja kulttuuriperintöprosessina. Paikallisen historiapolitiikan tarkastelua." *Kulttuuripolitiikan Tutkimuksen Vuosikirja* 1 (1): 56–69. https://doi.org/10.17409/kpt.v1i1.106

Sivula, Anna. 2017. "Kulttuurisen muistin kätkemä konflikti: Paikallista muistomerkkihanketta koskevat uutisten kommenttiketjut negatiivisen kulttuuriperinnön tilana." In *Rajaamatta. Etnologisia keskusteluja*, edited by Hanneleena Hieta, Aila Nieminen, Maija Mäki, Katriina Siivonen Katriina, and Timo J. Virtanen Timo, 315–348. Helsinki: Ethnos.

Smith, Laurajane. 2006. *Uses of Heritage*. London: Routledge.

Smith, Laurajane. 2021. *Emotional Heritage*. London: Routledge.

Suominen, Jaakko, Anna Sivula, and Maria B. Garda. August 2018. "Incorporating Curator, Collector and Player Credibilities: Crowdfunding Campaign for the Finnish Museum of Games and the Creation of Game Heritage Community." *Kinephanos – Canadian Journal of Media Studies*, Special Issue Preserving Play (edited by Alison Gazzard and Carl Therrien). https://www.kinephanos.ca/2018/incorporating-curator-collector-and-player-credibilities-crowdfunding-campaign-for-the-finnish-museum-of-games-and-the-creation-of-game-heritage-community/

Tahkokorpi, Tuuli. June 4, 2020." Legendaarinen Pekka-peli vedettiin pois myynnistä – valmistajalle sateli asiattomia yhteydenottoja." *Iltalehti.* https://www.iltalehti.fi/kotimaa/a/014c4f38-5bed-4fbb-abbd-c9d9111b769a

Thomas, S. E., Herva, V.-P., Seitsonen, O., and Koskinen-Koivisto, E. 2019. "Dark Heritage." In *Encyclopedia of Global Archaeology*, edited by C. Smith. Living Edition Cham: Springer.

Turun Sanomat. September 21, 2005. https://www.ts.fi/viihde/1074070078.

Uusihakala, Katja. 2007. *Afrikan tähti – pelilaudan kääntöpuoli.* Helsinki: Helinä Rautavaaran museo.

Vettenniemi, Erkki. May 5, 1998. "Orjarannikon vangit." *Helsingin Sanomat.* https://www.hs.fi/kulttuuri/art-2000003713876.html

Walsh, Kevin. 1992. *The Representation of the Past: Museums and Heritage in the Postmodern World.* London: Routledge.

108   *A. Sivula and J. Suominen*

Waterton, Emma, and Steve Watson. 2015. "Heritage as a Focus of Research: Past, Present and New Directions." In *The Palgrave Handbook of Contemporary Heritage Research*, edited by Emma Waterton, Steve Watson, 1–17. Basingstoke: Palgrave Macmillan.

Wieland, Heiko, Kaisa Koskela-Huotari, Kaisa, and Stephen L. Vargo. 2016. "Extending Actor Participation in Value Creation: An Institutional View." *Journal of Strategic Marketing* 24: 210–226. https://doi.org/10.1080/0965254X.2015.1095225

Ylänen, Henna. 2017. "Kansakunta pelissä. Nationalismi ja konfliktit 1900-luvun alun suomalaisissa lautapeleissä." *Ennen ja nyt* 1/2017. https://journal.fi/ennenjanyt/article/view/108787/63784

Yle News. October 21, 2021. https://yle.fi/news/3-12151820

8 No Meeples for *Scramble for Africa*

Online Debates on Playing Historical Trauma

Natàlia Lozano-Monterrubio

Juan Luis Gonzalo-Iglesia

Núria Araüna-Baró

Introduction

In 2019, after receiving fierce criticism on social networks and specialist on-line forums such as BoardGameGeek, the publisher GMT Games announced the withdrawal of *Scramble for Africa*, still in a prototype phase. GMT's spokesperson alleged that: "It's clear to me that the game is out of step with what most Eurogame players want from us, in terms of both topic and treatment" and highlighted that players' comments had led them to reconsider its publication (GMT Games, 2019). The aim of this paper is to analyze the online controversies about colonialism (in the past and in its 'neo' form) to observe the emergence in analog gamer culture of what Spivak (1999) termed the "postcolonial subject." We sustain that "postcolonial subject" has become a participant in public discussion through a savvy use of social media, and that it broadens the traditionally white and masculine geek gamer culture (Trammell, 2022). We study how the discussion around colonial legacies, playable representations, and the game industry show different strategies through which individuals position themselves to collective trauma.

Colonial Debates in Contemporary Cultures of Playability

Postcolonial studies tackle the socioeconomic, legal, and cultural remains of imperial regimes that sustained "institutional colonialism" and the subsequent power relationships generated by or surviving after their collapses (Gikandi, 1996). Unequal relationships informed by the recent past are pervasive in economic and sociocultural relationships, and the descendants of the colonized and oppressed people still carry their material marks in their bodies and

DOI: 10.4324/9781003356318-8

histories (Trammell, 2022). These unbalanced positions are routinely legitimized in cultural representations in books, popular music, films, TV series or games. In this regard, taking a postcolonial stance allows us to point at the biases that reproduce neocolonial understandings of the past and the present, and to reflect on how we could build a decolonial future (Albrecht, 2019). This does not deny that the postcolonial approach is in itself subject to debates about its "post" (structuralist) ways of reproducing the old binaries between the Europeans and "others" (Chibber, 2013). Drawing from the Marxist anticolonial thinkers of the 1950s and 1960s (Brennan, 2006), postcolonial theorists have developed a complex, sometimes polyphonic framework to tackle colonial prejudice.

Controversies about colonialism are common around many cultural products, also in games that translate the historical imaginary of the past into playable items (Borit et al., 2018). These representations of the past are based on recurring topics, often trivialized, which are recognizable by players. Murray suggests that games have been looked at primarily through the lenses of technology and playability, and highlights that a postcolonial perspective might be of critical worth if it can work "against the grain of profit-and innovation-driven discourses in games" (2018:4). In this light, even relatively abstract games such as the popular *Minecraft* can be read as normalizing capitalist extractivism and expansionism (Dooghan, 2019). The recent popularization of board games has raised academic interest (Booth, 2021) for some of those debates, previously held on videogames. At the same time, the board games market has been expanding. Specifically, within historical games, there has been a trend toward hybridizing complex historical game designs and more playable Eurogame forms (Woods, 2012) that tend to make a more abstract use of history.

A deeper critique of game design as carrying the "perspective of the colonizer" (Borit et al., 2018) aligns with Spivak's claim (1988) for the impossibility of the subaltern to speak (for us "to play, or be played"), and thus the impossibility of telling history on its own terms. Put in another way, Mukherjee (2018, 13) reflects that, also in games, the images of the Orient are always manufactured and only represent what colonial imperialism wishes to show and see. Norcia (2019) showed how the eighteenth-century British board games for children were consciously designed as imperial management training tools. However, Robinson (2014) asserts that even the conflict-avoidance structure of Eurogames such as *Catan* (KOSMOS, 1995) may result in the invisibilization of colonial violence and produce a vision of colonization without conflict, with no native populations or ethnocide. There have been board games looking for alternate perspectives on colonialism and history, such as *This Guilty Land* (Hollandspiele, 2018). Yet, speaking of videogames – and we could say the same about analog games – Mukherjee (2018) contends that, even when intending to offer alternative versions of history, they end up "replacing one elite with another, effectively tying into the logic that they seek to overturn" (14).

Postcolonial Players' Debates Online

Beyond recognizing that playable history might erase some of the problematic aspects of the past (e.g. extreme violence and massive deaths in slave transportation) or legitimize historical exploitation, we want to focus on how more concerned understandings of history emerge in players' conversations. Even if Höglund (2008) asserted that players and reviewers are more interested in the dynamics and narrative of games than in their politics, our case study shows the emerging centrality of political debates. Since one of the concerns of postcolonial studies is "the constant repetition of White European and American values and tropes (…) linked to the seductive and pleasurable aspects of global capitalism" (Trammell, 2022), we aim at observing what tensions arise between the experience of these pleasures and ethical approaches to play, and how these tensions are expressed online. Authors such as Jayanth (2021) and Trammell (2022) have stated how the European colonizer thought, ingrained in the mechanics of play, promotes empathy for the colonizers through incarnating their mechanics and rewarding the practices of exploitation and subjugation. But is this the only possibility?

Specialized online forums offer new opportunities for expanded dialogue between players of diverse backgrounds, game designers, and publishing companies. This way, we can better understand the possibilities of history-telling ingrained in board games, and the critical responses to it that arise from the collision between a cultural artifact (here, the prototype of *Scramble for Africa*) and its context. As we will see, Höglund's assumption (2008) that board game players are less politically aware than other cultural consumers is challenged when confronted with online discussions. Social networks have opened up a space for discussion where postcolonial diasporas can express their views (Franklin, 2001) and disseminate concerns for fairer views of the past, plus the need for reparation. The "postcolonial subject" (Spivak, 1999), as multiple as it is, is here a subject of enunciation, successful in building alliances to decenter board game worldviews: "the most profound way any of us can resist the colonial tropes embedded in play theory is to read, learn, and understand what the legacy of colonialism means for those who have lived through it and their descendants" (Trammell, 2022).

As Mukherjee (2018) observes, players' do not necessarily share the cultural values represented in a game and, depending on their position and ideology, might "actualize" what we understand as the postcolonial experience. The interactive structure of games guides players' construction of meaning and their understanding of historical momentum (Kapell and Elliot, 2013). Despite this, this guidance does not foreclose interpretative freedom and the ability to ultimately transgress games' narratives. In this sense, the decisions that players take in a game are diverse (represent a role, take strategic decisions, test what is not permitted in the real world, etc.). Holl et al. (2020) consider that a game can be read as a continuous iteration of decisions, some of which with a moral load. We sustain that this requirement of continuous decision-making promotes processes of reflection which expand in-game conversations (Gonzalo and Araüna, 2018). Through verbal or performative expressions during the game, players suspend the tale offered by the game and may counteract it through their own knowledge and ideological position (Mukherjee, 2018). The game can thus be understood as an interactive experience with history, but also as a space of dialogue and reflection during the game or beyond. This is especially relevant for digital media as venues of public conversation. Online forums, social networking sites, and online video servers are platforms where players may propose interpretations or participate in games' oppositional interpretive frameworks. As Sedelmeier and Baum (2022) highlight, numerous online debates about colonialism generated among the board game community indicate that "there is an interest in critical questions about the action framework of games not only among Lugologists and Cultural Scientists, but also among the players themselves" (97). Moreover, players may contend online about how they feel affected by the relationship of the simulation experience to their personal experience and genealogy.

The Flight of *Scramble for Africa*

On 20 February 2019, GMT Games, mostly known as a wargame publisher, announced the launch of the prototype of the board game *Scramble for Africa* in their P500 preorder system. The information released at that moment was minimal, just an outline of the setting: the exploration and colonization of Africa during the nineteenth century. The game achieved 300 cut orders during its first month, even before the designer included more information. Even if the data was scarce, it seemed that the game format would be close to a Eurogame, in which playability is a priority.

Despite its promising appearance, the prototype started to receive fierce criticism on social media, especially on BoardGameGeek (BGG), a digital database and one of the main forums of board games with more than two million registered users (BGG, 2021a). This webpage is considered the most significant source of information on gaming, and besides reviews and play-aids, it contains a forum section. These forums are moderated in order to warrant an inclusive conversation, free of racist, homophobic, misogynistic, and transphobic comments (BGG, 2021b). In April, GMT editors announced the withdrawal of *Scramble for Africa*, even if previous board games on colonialism such as *Source of Nile* (Avalon Hill, 1978), *Heart of Africa* (Phalanx Games, 2004), *Colonialism* (Spielworxx, 2013) or *Mombasa* (eggertspiele, 2015) had been released without public controversy.

Our research examines the discourses that emerged on BoardGameGeek (BGG) in the first quarter of 2019. In those days, users generated five different forums on *Scramble for Africa* which overall contained 1002 posts (Table 8.1). However, the moderator deleted 316 posts (which equals 31.5

Table 8.1 Number of posts (total and deleted) within the selected forums

Forum title	Number of posts per forum	Number of deleted posts by the moderator
Scramble for Africa	120 posts	0 posts
The Designer did nothing wrong!	202 posts	68 posts
I thought we were past this	457 posts	190 posts
Further game description from the GMT blog – webcache	75 posts	6 posts
How about a new and better Publisher?	148 posts	52 posts
Total number	**1002 posts**	**316 posts**

percent of the total) because these infringed BGG community rules that try to respect different opinions and preserve gender, racial and sexual diversity (BGG 2021b). Therefore, the total number of available public posts is 686.

We analyzed these conversations during August 2021 by following Braun and Clarke's (2006) guide for thematic analysis methodology. The analysis examined 350 posts (51 percent of the data corpus) corresponding to users that had intervened three or more times in the forums. The posts correspond to 90 different users (with three or four posts each). In the first stage, we transferred all 350 selected contributions into a text document and familiarized ourselves with the data. Then, each researcher analyzed the first 80 posts manually using the line-by-line technique, which helped to identify theory-driven codes and build a preliminary coding framework. Once codes were agreed upon and naturalized by all researchers, the coding framework was applied to the remaining forum contributions but was constantly revised (in a constant-comparison approach) that merged similar codes and created new ones when it was thought appropriate. In the analysis, we asked how participants positioned themselves in front of colonialism as a game narrative, how they debate between morality and freedom to play any game, and what they expect from the game industry. Finally, codes were grouped into three main themes: postcolonial players' positions; users' agency, and game industry.

Can We Play Colonialism? Perspectives and Players

Playing colonialism is one of the main topics debated in the forums, beyond how the specific discourses, maps or representations of this historical process are made. Results show different user perspectives concerning the suitability of playing *Scramble for Africa*. We have identified four types of players that range from those who are against playing traumatic episodes of history to those who express enthusiasm about these themes and the re-enactment of power inequalities. In the middle of these antagonist positions, there is a group who considers that colonialism and postcolonialism consequences should be represented under some conditions, as the topic generates public thoughtful debate. We have categorized their positions as: ethical players, critical players, ludic players, and guilty-pleasure players. As all categorizations, ours have an abstract condition and there are individuals who might have traits of more than one, but they serve us as frames to systematize the debate.

The first group, ethical players, broadly condemns board games based on colonial processes under the assumption that historical trauma should not be playable or enjoyable. This position would adhere with Trammell's notion (2022) that commercial board games are necessarily embedded in colonial thought patterns. Thus, some users passionately support the cancellation of *Scramble for Africa*:

> I'm someone who thinks there are very few topics that should not be games. This is very close to that line [...] I don't wish to be hyperbolic, but what I see here is barely a step above a train game about the Holocaust in terms of tastelessness
>
> (user 23).

Ethical players tend to blame the rest of the users as insensitive for their inability to empathize with those who suffer or are descendants of the oppressed. The debate could be summarized in this post:

> User x states: Everyone affected is long dead.
>
> User y replies: A billion Africans might have a different view.
>
> (user 13).

Even if gamers recognize that consuming representations of exploitation does not turn people into colonial advocates, they warn against the dangers of normalizing biased views of history: "White supremacism is a thing, and while it looks pretty trivial, I could argue that a badly designed game about colonialism could reinforce ideas that white exploitation of Africa was harmless or even beneficial" (user 19). In consequence, ethical players consider that the industry should avoid the publication of more colonialist games. For them, changing the setting of *Scramble for Africa* would solve the problem. This reveals the importance that ethical players give to "themes":

> Seriously. Set it on Mars or with exploding Caticorns and this game works just fine without leaning into slavery and prompting players to grog nards over who can optimize colonialist and genocidal strategies the best
>
> (user 54).

The second group, critical players, admits the uneasiness and danger of colonial representations of the past. However, they consider that these games enhance a public debate and the development of social consciousness of an oppressive and unfair past. They understand players as reflexive actors with the capacity to interpret and transgress the represented world. Some even consider these games pedagogical as they raise discussion and thoughtful thinking about colonialism and other practices of oppression, creating a possibility for empathy (Spivak, 2012).

> Any cultural product is not necessarily interpreted in the way the designer/sender wishes. […] Take Tintin in the Congo for instance. That can be used in many ways. […] In some places, it's banned because it's racist and in other places, it's used to educate on how racist society was not too long ago
>
> (user 26).

> To me this is shaky ground on which to situate an argument for why a game shouldn't exist; I'd almost go so far as to argue that it's an argument for such a game. […] Games permit one form of structured inquiry into such questions
>
> (user 29).

Critical players want to talk about traumatic topics in a conscious way. However, oftentimes their arguments end up being accused by ethical players of whitewashing history. On occasions, critical players must reaffirm their positions:

> Colonialism as a theme for board games should be discussed. Critically […]. If a game has a colonialist setting, even if players are supposed to represent colonial powers, it does not mean that anyone involved in creating, publishing, or playing the game sees colonialism as harmless or glosses over it
>
> (user 58).

Ludic players, the third group, consist of users that believe that a game should not be compared to real-life standards and defend that simulation and playability must be free from ethical constraints. Some uphold the idea that games should be dissociated from history. Despite this, it does not imply that the entertainment of the game makes them insensitive to colonialism itself.

> IT IS A GAME. […] And from what I gather the theme is offensive to some. But how many games do we all play that have TERRIBLE themes if you think about? […] Does playing a game justify murder? No. Does playing a game with a theme like war, slavery or pillaging justify those acts in history? No!
>
> (user 17).

This group of players defends the idea that everyone is free to choose what they want to play, despite its topic and ideological position, and disagrees with what they see as "impositions" that try to repair faults from the past. On occasions, tensions between ethical players and ludic ones are evident, as the latter group seems to perceive they are being told what could and could not be played:

> We need to ban *Puerto Rico* and *Mombasa* while we are at it, I guess? Also, my version of *Five Tribes* has the original slave cards, should I throw that away as well?
>
> (user 11).

Lastly, if some board games simulating historical oppression and violence have succeeded, it is due to the fourth category of (silent) players that we have termed guilty-pleasure ones. This figure recognizes the unethical pleasure of "playing" cruel dynamics of history by perpetrating "politically incorrect" atrocities like enslaving and slaughtering people. There is a strong sense of irony in the discourses of these players, and – common with ludic players – a clear separation between the pleasures of playing and the workings of real life. We see this category, even more, reluctant to discourse regulation than ludic players, as potentially aligned with the resurgence of an imperial nostalgia that labels every call for colonial consciousness as "woke" (Mitchell, 2021). However, this fourth category appears timidly in just one of the posts. Researchers suspect that some of their comments may have appeared among the 316 posts deleted by the moderator for attempting BGG's community rules that are intended to preserve gender, racial and sexual diversity (BGG, 2021b). The post that supports the designer and uses black humor to defend the game includes references to the pop-culture novel *Heart of Darkness* by Joseph Conrad:

> I hope the designer sees it, […] don't give up hope, you did nothing wrong! […] I totally would have bought this game and played it wearing a pith helmet drinking gin and tonics until the quinine made my ears ring. Hope it sees the light of day so we can journey into the heart of darkness! The horror, the horror!
>
> (user 10).

Context Matters: Other Sides of the Debate

Apart from the intrinsic ethical constraints of players about whether colonialism should be playable or not, or under which conditions, the debate shows underlying tensions related to the economic dimension of games as a cultural product.

In hobby board games, there are several genres (i.e., thematic games, abstracts, euros, or wargames). Most of the specialized participants of BGG are aware of these differences, and some use them as an explanation for how the representation of history should be understood according to genre specificity. While wargames focus on the historical simulation of an event or period and are supposed to deepen into complex topics, Eurogames instead use the historical moment as a catchy setting for its narrative and rely on playability and ludic mechanics. They aim at two market niches: wargames are addressed to knowledgeable audiences, whose interests lie in learning about historical momentum, whereas Eurogames are targeted to family publics who look for entertaining leisure. The difference between these genres has a direct effect on the treatment of colonialism in terms of depth and reality, and some users justify that *Scramble for Africa* barely addresses the underlying history based on its category/genre:

This wasn't going to be a simulation wargame that sought to show what happened or how it could have happened differently. This was a Euro, where your goal is generally to optimize an engine to efficiently generate points

(user 49).

Besides, some users raised the fact that they cannot give their judgments about the game, which had not even been released, with the scarce published information. They give the benefit of goodwill to the game, as even in those cases where the games are published and information is fully available, it is not until the moment of playing when the mechanics and dynamics complete the gaming experience:

I myself felt offended by *Labyrinth: The War on Terror, 2001 –?* for many years, and it was not until I played the game that I discovered the true intention of the designer – that being the use of a game to explain historical motivations and interactions between two very different groups. So, maybe this game will be terrible, or maybe it will be great. It's too soon to judge in my opinion

(user 22).

Some users expressed that their deception about *Scramble for Africa* is not the game itself but the publisher. GMT Games specializes in wargames – the fact that they decided to create a Eurogame with a plain narrative offended its loyal customers, who see their publisher sold to commercial decisions.

Board games are a serious medium, and they deserve serious literary discussion, especially GMT which has a record of doing an incredibly good job with their settings and presenting historical research. This game is a fiasco for them

(user 28).

GMT have publicly stated that the Euro games are the fastest-growing section of their catalogue. [...] The point is GMT's core audience may not be wargamers in the near future

(user 51).

This last point leads us to another debate related to users' agency and freedom. Since the emergence of social media, the market is not only regulated by the law of supply and demand but also by the opinions shared by customers on their social media, as they have the power to shape the enterprises' reputation (Scott, 2009). Seeing this, the debate focuses on whether the cancellation of *Scramble for Africa* was an act of censorship or a free market. On the one hand, many users feel annoyed that the opinions of a minority led to the withdrawal of the game, and they advocate self-regulation of the free market: "In the end, I believe no game is too taboo that it can't be published; one man's trash may be another's cup of tea. [...] People who are sensitive [to these topics] could speak with their wallets" (user 2). Some members go further and blame today's cancel culture: "People try to force their opinions about what's right or wrong on others by running campaigns that aim to prevent products from being made and to ruin the companies that are trying to make them. It's vigilantism, public enforced censorship" (user 57). Members are also concern about these online campaigns as these occur with increasing frequency and put pressure on designer and publisher decisions: "This is happening with increasing regularity in the book world, [...] perhaps I shouldn't be surprised that it's happening in the game world too" (user 60). To fight against GMT's final resolution, some users encourage others to boycott the publisher and ask the designer to self-publish: "I urge Joe Chacon to Kickstart and self-publish this game. Even at a higher price for a smaller print run. You will find many people willing to back as a protest against censorship" (user 39).

On the other hand, other members defend that the cancellation of the game was part of the free market as it answered GMT's business resolutions after reading users' opinions: "A business chose to listen to some feedback from the intended audience and chose not to publish something, which is always their prerogative" (user 35). These users also complain that it seems that colonialism and other topics related with historical traumas seem to be taboo even in the forums as they are easily labeled as "censorship" and mock over other users for using that term easily:

A funny thing about BGG is that we can complain about a game's mechanics, components, play length, player count, game weight, box size, [...], but the moment anyone objects to a theme for its evocation of historical atrocities or for any other personal ethical reasons, it's suddenly considered "censorship" and "snowflake pandering" and "oversensitive Social Justice Warrior" bullshit

(user 3).

Call it censorship if you want, though know that it absolutely isn't. You probably have an easy life if the closest thing to actual censorship that you've ever experienced is a board game company choosing not to publish a board game

(user 48).

Conclusions

This chapter focused on a representative case of how collective debates and reflections over postcoloniality have transformed the way in which games and play are approached. Overall, these debates illuminate how part of the white masculine gaming culture is being cracked by "postcolonial subjects" (Spivak, 2012) and anticolonial allies. If white men and eurocentric publishers had been hegemonic in (global) game design and play, the diversification of players and workers in the industries is leading to a more complex positionality. This research has stressed the role of the player and the interpreter of the games more generally as an active agent who interacts with known and unknown peers through social networks. At the same time, results have challenged former studies that pointed to the unawareness of players regarding the political dimension of gaming (Höglund, 2008). Nowadays, debates on the reproduction of neocolonial frames on board and videogames are affluent at least on social media. Besides, online forums might be sites to forge consciousness and intervene in public opinion and market decisions. These debates are not isolated but situated within a dispute over the decolonization of history and memories, that have had meaningful expressions like throwing down statues of slave traders (Mitchell, 2021). With regards to games, we have observed how "ethical" players consider that it is not possible to play about a traumatic past event without reproducing colonial views. On their side, "critical" players would strive for more accurate and fair game design on these historical processes. "Guilty-pleasure" players and some "ludic" players would instead prefer freedom and so defend that responsibility for injustice is not to be charged upon games. In the context in which players demand progressive and inclusive politics through social networks, conservative groups seem to be appropriating "freedom of expression" discourses and blame critical voices for being repressive and leading to a woke cancel culture.

The *Scramble for Africa*, beyond contributing to this debate, has generated discussion in the game industry and has led to reflection about how the sector should be accountable to the past. Designers and users agree that board games have not traditionally portrayed the perspectives of the oppressed accurately but also recognize that the industry is timidly changing. Thus, in general terms, we can see that the controversy has made people aware of the need for more games on colonialism that give voice and agency to marginalized communities and their perspectives. Participants even suggested specific ideas addressed to publishers about how players would like to game with historical traumatic events like giving a more prominent role to subaltern groups, or building an overtly critical perspective on the past, as well as quoting counterexamples of games that have made an explicit anticolonial discourse, such as *Spirit Island* (Arrakis Games, 2017). The emergence of initiatives such as the Zenobia Awards, which seek to promote the inclusion of designers from groups underrepresented in the industry and encourages their visions – also projects such as *Free at Last* (The Dietz Foundation) and *Borikén: The Taíno Resistance* (GMT Games), which deal with traumatic and complex topics from the perspectives of the oppressed – are a step that shows the progressive consciousness of the sector or, at least, its reactivity to the public critique.

References

Albrecht, M. 2019. *Postcolonialism Cross-Examined. Multidirectional Perspectives on Imperial and Colonial Pasts and the Neocolonial Present.* Oxon: Routledge.

BGG. 2021a. "Welcome to BoardGameGeek." Last modified September 5, 2022. https://boardgamegeek.com/wiki/page/Welcome_to_BoardGameGeek.

BGG. 2021b. "BoardGameGeek Community Rules." Last modified September 5, 2022. https://boardgamegeek.com/community_rules#toc1.

Booth, P. 2021. *Board Games as Media.* London: Bloomsbury Academic.

Borit, C., Borit, M. and Olsen, P. 2018. "Representations of Colonialism in Three Popular, Modern Board Games: Puerto Rico, Struggle of Empires and Archipelago." *Open Library of Humanities* 4(1): 17, 1–40. https://doi.org/10.16995/olh.211.

Braun, V. and Clarke, V. 2006. "Using Thematic Analysis in Psychology." *Qualitative Research in Psychology* 3(2): 77–101. https://doi.org/10.1191/1478088706qp063oa.

Brennan, T. 2006. "From Development to Globalization: Postcolonial Studies and Globalization Theory." In N. Lazarus (Ed.), *The Cambridge Companion to Postcolonial Literary Studies.* Cambridge: Cambridge University Press.

Chibber, V. 2013. *Postcolonial Theory and the Specter of Capital.* London: Verso Books.

Dooghan, D. 2019. "Digital Conquerors: Minecraft and the Apologetics of Neoliberalism." *Games and Culture* 14(1): 67–86. https://doi.org/10.1177/1555412016655678.

Franklin, M. I. 2001. "Inside Out: Postcolonial Subjectivities and Everyday Life Online." *International Feminist Journal of Politics* 3(3): 387–422. https://doi.org/10.1080/14616740110078194

Gikandi, S. 1996. *Maps of Englishness: Writing Identity in the Culture of Colonialism.* New York: Columbia University Press.

GMT Games. 2019. "P500 Update: Removing Scramble for Africa." Accessed September 5, 2022. https://mailchi.mp/a9c2643ed89c/p500-update-removing-scramble-for-africa.

Gonzalo, J. and Araüna, N. 2018. "Digitalizando la experiencia analógica de juego: el caso de los juegos (post)coloniales." In D. Aranda, J. Sánchez-Navarro, and A. J. Planells (Eds.), *Game & Play: La Cultura del Juego Digital*. Camas, Sevilla: Egregius Ediciones, pp. 87–105.

Höglund, J. 2008. "Electronic Empire: Orientalism Revisited in the Military Shooter." *Games Studies* 8(1). http://gamestudies.org/0801/articles/hoeglund.

Holl, E., Bernard, S., and Melzer, A. 2020. "Moral Decision-Making in Video Games: A Focus Group Study on Player Perceptions." *Human Behavior and Emerging Technologies* 2(3): 278–287. https://doi.org/10.1002/hbe2.189.

Jayanth, M. 2021. "White Protagonism and Imperial Pleasures in Game Design #DIGRA21." *Medium*. https://medium.com/@betterthemask/white-protagonism-and-imperial-pleasures-in-game-design-digra21-a4bdb3f5583c

Kapell, M. W. and Elliott, A. B. (Eds.) 2013. *Playing with the Past: Digital Games and the Simulation of History*, Bloomsbury Publishing.

Mitchell, P. 2021. "Sovereign bodies." In *Imperial nostalgia*. Manchester: Manchester University Press.

Mukherjee, S. 2018. "Playing Subaltern: Video Games and Postcolonialism." *Games and Culture* 13(5): 504–520. https://doi.org/10.1177/1555412015627258.

Murray, S. 2018. "The Work of Postcolonial Game Studies in the Play of Culture." *Open Library of Humanities* 4(1): 13. https://doi.org/10.16995/olh.285.

Norcia, M. A. 2019. *Gaming Empire in Children's British Board Games, 1836–1860* (1st ed.). London: Routledge.

Robinson, W. 2014. "Orientalism and Abstraction in Eurogames." *Analog Game Studies* 1(5). https://analoggamestudies.org/2014/12/orientalism-and-abstraction-in-eurogames/

Scott, D. M. 2009. *The New Rules of Marketing and PR. How to use News Releases, Blogs, Podcasting, Viral Marketing & Online Media to Reach Buyers Directly*. Hoboken: John Wiley & Sons.

Sedelmeier, T. and Baum, L. 2022. "The Controversity About Colonialism in Board Games—Illustrated by the Example of Santa Maria." In Edler, D., Kühne, O., and Jenal, C. (Eds.), *The Social Construction of Landscapes in Games*. RaumFragen: Stadt – Region – Landschaft. Wiesbaden: Springer.

Spivak, G. C. 1988. "Can the Subaltern Speak?." In Cary Nelson and Lawrence Grossberg (Eds.), *Marxism and the Interpretation of Culture*. Urbana, IL: University of Illinois Press.

Spivak, G. C. 1999. *A Critique of Postcolonial Reason. Toward a History of the Vanishing Present*. Cambridge, MA: Harvard University Press.

Spivak, G. C. January 20, 2012. "Spivak on an Aesthetic Education in the Era of Globalization." YouTube video, 4:48. https://youtu.be/YBzCwzvudv0 [Last accessed 2 November 2022].

Trammell, A. 2022. "Decolonizing Play." *Critical Studies in Media Communication* 39(3): 239–246. https://doi.org/10.1080/15295036.2022.2080844

Woods, S. 2012. *Eurogames. The Design, Culture and Play of Modern European Board Games*. Jefferson, NC: McFarland & Company.

References – games

eggertspiele, *Mombasa*. Analog game designed by Alexander Pfister, 2015.

Arrakis Games, *Spirit Island*. Analog game designed by R. Eric Reuss, 2017.

Phalanx Games, *Heart of Africa*. Analog game designed by Andreas Steding, 2004.

Avalon Hill, *Source of the Nile*. Analog game designed by Ross Maker and Dave Wesely, 1978.

Hollandspiele, *This Guilty Land*. Analog game designed by Amabel Holland, 2018.

KOSMOS, *Catan*. Analog game designed by Klaus Terber, 1995.

Spielworxx, *Colonialism*. Analog game designed by Scott W. Leibbrandt, 2013.

Index

Mexican identity 57–58;
foundational myths 59; identity
of contemporary Mexico 61–63;
Mesoamerican heritage 68–70;
traditional board games 63–64;
unearthing the Mesoamerican
heritage 67–68; World of
contradictions 60–61
Mexican Trading Card Games (TCG) 66
Microcosmos (2019) 66
Mignolo, W. 77
Miranda, J. 40
Mochocki, M. 54, 70
Mombasa (2015) 110
Moneta Games 66
Mukherjee, S. 1, 2, 4, 6–7, 12, 53, 54,
57, 80, 110–111
Murray, J. 28
Murray, S. 45, 68
Musta Pekka (game) 96

Navegador (game) 48
Necronomicorp (2016) 66
Neuroriders (2022) 66
nondigital board games 1
Norcia, M. A. 110
Nummelin, J. 96, 97

Ofrendados (2021) 66, 68
Ollinkalli (2016) 66, 68
Orbanes, P. 40

Parashar, S. 21
Party Booster (2019) 66
Party Panda Pirates (2022) 66
Party Warriors (2019) 66
Patria Libre (2022) 66
Pátzcuaro (game) 68
Pax Pamir (game) 27, 29, 30
Peltomaa, M. 99
Penix-Tadsen, P. 80
Pikkujämsä, M. 101
Political Support Level (PSL) 31
Posada, J. G. 63
*Possessed by the Past: The Heritage
Crusade and the Spoils of
History* (1996) 92
postcolonial approach 1, 110
postcolonial game studies: annotated
bibliography 2–5; Brazilian
(gamer) culture 6; colonialist
and anti-colonialist in *Spirit
Island* 6; design elements 5;

heritagisation and heritage
conflict 6–7; Mexican board
games 6; *Scramble for Africa* 7;
video games and tabletop
role-playing games 7–8
*Postcolonial Perspectives in Game
Studies* (2018) 1
*The Problematic Pleasures of
Productivity and Efficiency in
Goa and Navegador* (2016) 3
Propaganda card 35
pure textual analysis 39

Rael, P. 39
Ramos, S. 63
Rampant exploitation 78
Rastas, A. 97
Reuss, R. E. 48–53
Reynolds, D. 47
The Road to Dien Bien Phu (2022) 14
Robinson, W. 3, 110
Role-Playing Games (RPG) 66
Roll a Game Expo (game) 67
roll and write game *Aban!* (2022) 65
Rolling Farmers (2021) 65
Romero, J. 40
Rossi, L. 96
Ruhnke, V. 18, 33, 35, 36, 40
Run that I'll catch you (game) 63

Salles, R. 77, 78
Salmi, H. 100
Scramble for Africa 109, 112–114, 118;
colonial debates 109–110;
debates 116–119; flight of
112–113; gaming experience
117; GMT's core audience
118; hobby board games 116;
number of posts **113**; overview
109; playing colonialism
113–116; postcolonial players'
debates online 111–112
Seat Wars (2018) 66
Sedelmeier, T. 112
Serpents and Snakes (game) 63, 64
The Settlers of Catan (game) 3, 47, 84
Shalev, I. 1
Shining Path: The Struggle for Peru
(1999) 30, 40
Sivula, A. 6–8
Smith, L. 8
Sonnleitner, M. W. 20
Source of Nile (1978) 110

For Product Safety Concerns and Information please contact our EU
representative GPSR@taylorandfrancis.com
Taylor & Francis Verlag GmbH, Kaufingerstraße 24, 80331 München, Germany

.